IBN BAJJAH'S
'ILM AL-NAFS

English Translation and Notes
By
M.S. Hasan Ma'sumi
M.A. Ph.D.

KITAB BHAVAN
New Delhi-110002

KITAB BHAVAN
Publishers, Distributors, Exporters & Importers
1784, Kalan Mahal, Darya Ganj,
New Delhi - 1100 02 (India)

Phones : (91-11) 23277392/93, 23274686, 32906494
Fax : (91-11) 23263383
Website : www.kitabbhavan.com
Email : nasri@vsnl.com
: nusrat@bol.net.in

3rd Edition 2009

ISBN : 81-7151-142-2
Book Code : I00429

Printed & Published in India by :
Nusrat Ali Nasri for KITAB BHAVAN
1784, Kalan Mahal, Darya Ganj,
New Delhi - 1100 02 [India]

PREFACE

Ibn Bājjah's *Kitāb al-Nafs* is now ready for the English readers. The Arabic text with the Arabic version of the Introduction and Notes prepared by the writer himself was sent to the "Revue de l' academie Arabe de Damas", Syria, long after the English translation together with the Arabic Text was submitted for publication to the Pakistan Historical Society of Karachi. The Arabic version, however, came out in the Arab World before the original work could see the light of the day.

In the year 1950, when the writer was in Oxford to do some research work in the field of Arabic Philosophy under the kind supervision of Dr. R. Walzer, the latter very kindly mentioned the Bodleian manuscript of Ibn Bājjah to the writer and advised him to select a portion thereof with a view to collate the same with the corresponding portion of the only other available manuscript in Berlin. After the treatise in hand was selected by the writer and approved by the authorities concerned, it was discovered that the Berlin manuscript would not be available, as it was lost in the last Great World War.

It was only through the valuable criticism of Prof. S. Van Den Berg, the encouragement and kind care of Sir H. A. R. Gibb, and the very effective supervision of Dr. R. Walzer that the writer succeeded in completing the edition which was submitted to the University of Oxford under the title "IBN BĀJJAH'S PARAPHRASE OF ARISTOTLE'S *DE ANIMA*" for the Degree of D. Phil. in 1952-53.

On the recommendation of Professor Paul Kahle, who visited Pakistan in 1956, the Pakistan Historical Society approved this small book to be included in its series of publications.

The writer feels deeply indebted to the above-mentioned distinguished orientalist and to the office-bearers and members of the Pakistan Historical Society through whose kind encouragement, supervision and assistance this work is now in the hands of the readers.

The writer also records his deep indebtedness to Dr. Serajul Huq, Head of the Department of Arabic and Islamic Studies; to Professor S. M. Hossain, former Head of the Department, and ex-Vice-Chancellor, University of Dacca; and to the University of Dacca, for their help, encouragement and grant of Study Advance.

In the end, the writer also offers sincere thanks and gratitude to Dr. Beeston (now the Laudean Professor of Arabic in Oxford), and other Assistants in the Oriental Section, Bodleian Library, Oxford; to Dr. S. Moinul Haq, General Secretary and Director of Research, Pakistan Historical Society, Karachi; to the proof reader, printer, and assistants of the Society; for their very kind assistance in preparing the work, and bringing it out of the press.

M. S. H.

CONTENTS

Introduction :

		Page
I.	The Subject	1
II.	The Manuscript	10

Translation :

			Page
Ch.	I.	On the Soul	13
,,	II.	Discourse on the Nutritive Faculty ...	29
,,	III.	Discourse on the Faculties of Sense Perception	43
,,	IV.	Discourse on Sight	79
,,	V.	Discourse on Hearing	88
,,	VI.	Discourse on Smell	92
,,	VII.	Discourse on Taste	96
,,	VIII.	Discourse on Touch	98
,,	IX.	On Common Sense	103
,,	X.	Discourse on the Faculty of Imagination	106
,,	XI.	Discourse on the Reasoning Faculty ...	117

Notes :

			Page
		Introduction :	122
Ch.	I	On the Soul	125
,,	II.	Discourse on the Nutritive Faculty ...	143
,,	III.	Discourse on the Faculties of Sense Perception	157
,,	IV.	Discourse on Sight	172
,,	V.	Discourse on Hearing	176
,,	VI.	Discourse on Smell	178
,,	VII.	Discourse on Taste	181

			Page
Ch.	VIII.	Discourse on Touch	182
,,	IX.	On Common Sense	185
,,	X.	Discourse on the Faculty of Imagination	187
,,	XI.	Discourse on the Reasoning Faculty ...	192

Bibliography 195

Appendix 199

Index 203

INTRODUCTION

I—THE SUBJECT

THE subject of this volume is the first edition of Ibn Bājjah's *Kitāb al-Nafs* with an English translation and historico-philosophical notes. The second volume will present Ibn Bājjah's other psychological treatises.

Abū Bakr Muḥammad ibn Yaḥya ibn al-Sā'igh, known as Ibn Bājjah (d. 533/1138),[1] the fore-runner of Averroes, " the commentator *par excellence* ", has been unanimously regarded as one of the chief representatives of Arabic philosophy. He has been referred to by his contemporaries as the greatest exponent of Aristotelian philosophy after Ibn Sīnā', the Shaykh al-Ra'īs.[2] But the world has hitherto remained so inadequately informed of and acquainted with his works as to know only a few tractates and *Kitāb Tadbīr al-Mutawaḥḥid* which last has been known through its Hebrew translation to Europe since the Middle Ages.

There are only two manuscripts of Ibn Bājjah's works known, preserved in the libraries of Oxford and Berlin. I started reading Ibn Bājjah's *Kitāb al-Nafs* in Oxford with the hope of collating it with the Berlin manuscript which had been, as I learned afterwards from the Librarian of the Berlin Library and through the good services of Prof. P. E. Kahle, shifted to the Eastern zone of Germany during the World War II and lost. Now I have no other excuse for editing an Arabic text from a single manuscript, but the one which Mr. D. M. Dunlop offers in the beginning of his article entitled " Ibn Bājjah's Tadbīr al-Mutawaḥḥid " when he says : " If the difficulties and hazards involved in attempting to edit an Arabic text, particularly of an abstract character, from a single manuscript should have been pointed out, the reply was ready to hand that if the work were to be edited at all, it must be from the Bodleian manuscript and that alone."[3]

In these circumstances, I have had no choice but to decipher the whole manuscript which consists of 222 folios and to establish as far as possible the text of obscure passages with the help of parallels. The text of the *Kitāb al-Nafs* was originally complete but, later on, Ibn Bājjah's friend and disciple, al-Wazīr 'Abu'l-Ḥasan 'Ali Ibn al-'Imām[4] through whom his writings have survived, lost a few pages from the end of the book. Ibn al-'Imām himself has expressed his regret for this loss.[5] Ibn Ṭufayl also, in the preface to his famous philosophical romance, *Hayy Ibn Yaqẓān*, mentions that Ibn Bājjah's *Kitāb al-Nafs* and most of his works are incomplete.[6]

Kitāb al-Nafs—An Independent Work:

Like *Kitāb Tadbīr al-Mutawaḥḥid, Kitāb al-Nafs* is always referred to by the author himself in terms that clearly indicate that it is his original and independent work, while he refers to other works of his as notes or commentaries on the works of Aristotle.[7] *Kitāb al-Nafs* is evidently an original work and is neither a commentary nor a paraphrase. But since in the arrangement of contents, and in the exposition of the fundamental psychological theories, it is more or less in conformity with most of the second and third books of the *De Anima* of Aristotle, it is not entirely wrong to call it a paraphrase of Aristotle's *De Anima* composed by Ibn Bājjah.

Ibn Bājjah's Style :

An eloquent poet and a gifted musician of great repute[8] as he is, Ibn Bājjah's philosophical style is highly abstract and a little uneven and stereotype. But his favourite disciple, Ibn al-'Imām, holds a different opinion and admires the clearness and beauty of the expression of Ibn Bājjah.[9] *Kitāb al-Nafs* itself, no doubt, bears evidence that his expression in places is lucid and simple in character. Like al-Fārābi, on whose writings he chiefly depends, he tries to elucidate a problem in simple language, but often his attempt to do so renders it complicated and obscure—a fact he is fully conscious of; occasionally he regrets his inability to revise his writings for want of time.[10] Often his sentences are not correct according to the usual rules of Arabic syntax. Particularly the pronouns (ضمائر) do, very often, not agree in gender with the nouns referred to; the examples are too numerous to put the whole blame on the scribe, who himself being a learned Qāḍī and disciple of Ibn al-'Imām, must have taken all care in copying.[11] His junior contemporary, Ibn Ṭufayl, rightly remarks :[12]

وقد صرح هو نفسه بذلک وذکر ان المعنى المقصود برهانه فى رسالته الاتصال ليس يعطيه ذلک القول اعطاءً بينا الا بعد عسر و استکراه شديد، وان ترتيب عبارته فى بعض المواضع على غير الطريق الاکمل و لو اتسع له الوقت مال لتبديلها

" In his Epistle concerning the Union, he (Ibn Bājjah) himself explains and mentions that it would require a great deal of trouble and pains to express clearly what he had undertaken to prove, and, that the method which he had made use of in making himself clear, was not, in many places, so exact as it might have been, and, that he would have attempted, if he had time, to alter it."

His Influence on his Contemporaries :

Nevertheless, Ibn Bājjah's scholarship remarkably influenced some of his junior contemporaries, particularly Ibn Rushd and Ibn Ṭufayl. His writings exerted a great influence on the writings of Ibn Rushd who evidently wrote his جوامع (paraphrases of Aristotle's works, published with the exception of *Kitāb al-Hiss wa'l Maḥsūs* in Hyderabad under the title of (*Rasā'il Ibn Rushd*) after Ibn Bājjah's works collected by Ibn al-'Imām under the title *Majmū'at min Kalām al-Shaykh al'Imām al-Wazīr Abī Bakr Muḥammad Ibn Bājjat al-Andalusi* which contains, besides other works his commentary on Aristotle's *Physics, Meteorology,* and *Historia Animalium.* As a matter of fact, Ibn Rushd himself admits in his *Talkhīṣ Kitāb al-Nafs*[13] in so many words that what he has expressed concerning Mind is the view of Ibn Bājjah. Of course, sometimes Ibn Rushd re-examines and criticises the philosophical views propounded by al-Fārābi, Ibn Sīnā', and Ibn Bājjah as well.[14] The explanatory notes which I have added to the translation will throw some light on the indebtedness of Ibn Rushd to Ibn Bājjah.

Importance of Kitāb al-Nafs :

Ibn Bājjah's *Kitāb al-Nafs* is of great importance not only for the fact that it provides us with the source and background of Ibn Rushd, but also because it helps in filling up the gap between al-Fārābi and Ibn Rushd.

Aristotle's *De Anima* was translated into Arabic in the ninth century by Isḥāq Ibn Ḥunayn.[15] This Arabic version has never been, up-till now, edited, but a manuscript has recently been found in Istambul. Alexander of Aphrodisias wrote an abridgment of the *De Anima* (extant in Greek and Hebrew) which was commented by al-Fārābi,[16] but this commentary has not been traced. Besides, as stated by Ibn al-Nadīm, the commentaries of Themistius and Simplicius were available in Arabic.[17] Ibn al-Bitrīq seems to have been the first to write in Arabic a paraphrase (جوامع) of the *De Anima*. Several other treatises bearing the title of كتاب النفس are found in the *Fihrist* under Theophrastus (ثاؤفرسطس, p. 252), Alexander of Aphrodisias (الاسكندر الافروديسى, p. 253),[18] Themistius (ثامسطيوس, p. 253), Plutarch (فلوطرخس, p. 254),[19] and Ariston (ارسطن, p. 255), but no manuscript of the Arabic versions has hitherto been discovered. Aḥmad Fu'ād al-Ahwāni of Egypt has published along with Ibn Rushd's *Talkhīṣ Kitāb al-Nafs* an Arabic text entitled *Kitāb al-Nafs al-mansūb li 'Isḥāq*, which is evidently not a translation but an anonymous commentary of the *De Anima* probably written before Ḥunayn ; a Persian version of the same is available in the Bodleian Library, Oxford.[20]

So far no Arabic commentary of the *De Anima*, besides the one just mentioned, has ever appeared, and Ibn Bājjah's *Kitāb al-Nafs* seems to be the earliest text hitherto known that gives the gist of all the three books of the *De Anima*. In his book, Ibn Bājjah refers, besides Aristotle, to al-Fārābi, Alexander, Galen, Themistius and Plato also. Although Ibn Sīnā' is never mentioned by Ibn Bājjah, the following tribute paid to him by his favourite disciple, Ibn al-'Imām, bears evidence how highly admired by the intelligentsia of Spain Ibn Sīnā' must have been: (Fol.4A)[21]

ويشبه انه لم يكن بعد ابى نصر الفارابى مثله فى الفنون التى تكلم عليها من تلك العلوم , فانه اذا قرنت اقاويله فيها باقاويل ابن سينا و الغزالى و هما اللذان فتح عليهما بعد ابى نصر فى المشرق فى فهم تلك العلوم ، ودونا فيها ، بان لك الرجحان فى اقاويله و فى حسن فهمه لاقاويل ارسطو والثلاثة ائمة دون ريب و آتون ماجاء به من قبلهم من بارع الحكمة عن يقين يمتاز بدء اقاويلهم و يتواردون فيها مع السلف الكريم -

" We really think that after Abū Naṣr al-Fārābi there was no man like Ibn Bājjah for the elevated manner in which he wrote and spoke on those sciences ; for if we establish a comparison between his writings and those of Ibn Sīnā', and al-Ghazzāli, the two authors most promoted the study of that science in the East after al-Fārābi, we shall find the balance inclining rather on the side of Ibn Bājjah, especially if we bear in mind the clearness and beauty of his expression and his aptitude in penetrating the writings of Aristotle. Of these, however, there can be no doubt that the two above-mentioned philosophers were, together with Ibn Bājjah, those who united in themselves all the learning and all the talents of their predecessors, distinguishing themselves by the clearness of their dissertations, and competing in their works with the most celebrated philosophers of antiquity."

The Soul and its Faculties :

In his *Kitāb al-Nafs*, obviously after Aristotle, Ibn Bājjah defines soul as the first entelechy of the organized body, and describes the three major faculties of the soul, *viz*. the nutritive, the sensitive, the imaginative faculties, the rational faculty being treated in an analogous way. Soul, according to him, is an equivocal term and cannot, therefore, be defined in one and the same way. His enquiry into the soul mainly concerns the soul of the animals.

The Nutritive Faculty :

The nutritive faculty, defined as the first entelechy of the organized nutritive body, is assisted by two other faculties: the faculty of growth, and the faculty of reproduction. The function of the faculty of nutrition is to prepare substances in the nutrient body which are employed for the preservation of the body, its growth, and in the end, for reproduction. Just as the nutritive faculty turns food into a part of the body of the nutrient the reproductive faculty in the body reproduces a body of the species of the body. Since the mover of the reproductive faculty is an 'Active Mind', no confusion takes place in reproducing its relevant species. This reproduction corresponds to spontaneous generation from putrefaction, in non-reproductive lower animals.

The Sensitive Faculty:

The sensitive faculty, defined as the first entelechy of the organized sentient body, perceives the forms of the sensed things. This faculty has several senses, each having an organ ; and hence, Ibn Bājjah calls them souls[22]—these senses are sight, hearing, smell, taste, touch, the common-sense, and the moving faculty which has been mentioned[23] but not described and which, I think, is the faculty of appetition ("القوة النزوعيه), as Ibn Bājjah himself explains in a separate treatise. He explains there that the appetitive soul has three faculties : imaginative appetition, intermediate appetition, and rational appetition. The first two, according to him, are common to all animals, and hence, they look after themselves as well as their progeny. The third is peculiar to man alone.[24]

Unlike al-Fārābi, provided the Fuṣūs is rightly attributed to him,[25] and Ibn Sīnā',[26] he never uses the terms " external " and " internal " for the senses, nor does he mention " المصورة ", the representative, though he mentions " retention " (الحفظ) and ascribes it to the common-sense.[27]

But, how does perception take place ? Ibn Bājjah, like Aristotle, precisely explains that perception means the reception of the forms of the sensed things, and although form is wrapped up in matter, here " form " means just a pattern or an image, and is matter *per prius* only, while the matter of the sensed things is matter *per posterius*. Since the perceived form has some connection with its matter, we perceive it with all its material qualities.

The Imaginative Faculty :

Defined as the first entelechy of the organized imaginative body, the imaginative faculty is preceded by sensation which supplies its matter. Sensation and imagination have, therefore, been described as two kinds of the perception of the soul. But the difference between the two is obvious inasmuch as sensation is particular and imagination general. The imaginative faculty culminates in the reasoning faculty through which a man expresses himself to another man, and achieves as well as imparts knowledge.

In short, the soul, as described by Ibn Bājjah himself,[28] is an Active Faculty (القوة الفاعلة) dual in character, since when soul is said of the first entelechy it is a Passive Faculty (القوة المنفعلة), and when of the last entelechy an Active Faculty (القوة الفاعلة). The dualism of matter and form, mover and moved, action and passion, and first and last—so remarkable a characteristic of Aristotelian thought—forms a natural and indispensable basis of all the arguments Ibn Bājjah advances in this book.

In a separate treatise on the Rational Faculty Ibn Bājjah mentions " the Divine Gift " through which the rational soul sees " the Gift " itself just as it sees with the faculty of the eye the light of the sun through the light of the sun.[29] This "Gift ", he further says, is "the communion with the Active Intellect " (العقل الفعال).[30]

Apart from this treatise, he has several other treatises in which he deals with different aspects of the soul, especially on the Appetitive Soul ("النفس النزوعية), the awareness of the Active Intellect (الوقوف على العقل الفعال), the natural desire (ماهية" الشوق الطبيعى), etc., in which he seems to have built his own system to explain the problems of Mind, prophecy, and revelation.

Thus I may conclude that Ibn Bājjah starts describing " Aristotelian psychology " and arrives, in the end, at the conclusion—the problem of prophecy—arrived at by Ibn Sīnā' and which has been dealt with in his *Mishkāt al-'Anwār* by 'Imām Ghazzāli whose name Ibn Bājjah mentions with respect and reverence.[31]

In the commentary an attempt has been made to provide materials to facilitate the understanding of the text. Besides quoting parallels from Ibn Bājjah himself, I have tried to trace the origin of his views in the works of Aristotle, al-Fārābi, Ibn Sīnā', and other Greek and Muslim philosophers.

As I am not well up in Greek, I have relied on the Oxford translation of the works of Aristotle and the English translation of other Greek works.

II—THE MANUSCRIPT

IBN Bājjah's *Kitāb al-Nafs* forms part of the Bodleian manuscript Pocock 206 entitled *Majmū'āt min Kalām al-Shaykh al-'Imām al-'Ālīm al-Kāmil al-Fāḍil al-Wazīr . . . Wazīr Abī Bakr Muḥammad Ibn Bājjat al-Andalusi.* The written pages of this manuscript of 222 folios is measured 3¾″ × 7½″, each page containing 27 and very often 32 lines. The date of the transcription given on folio 120A indicates that this manuscript was written by al-Qāḍī al-Ḥasan Ibn Muḥammad Ibn Muḥammad Ibn Muḥammad Ibn al-Naḍar at Qūṣ in the month of *Rabi*, 11, 547/1152 and was collated with the original copy of Ibn al-'Imām which the latter had read with the author and had finished reading on *Ramaḍān* 15, 530/1135, i.e. nearly three years before the death of Ibn Bājjah. This notice, by the way, settles that Ibn Bājjah died in the year 533/1138, i.e. after 530/1135 and not in 525/1130.[32] Another date has been given at the end of Fol. 118A ; it confirms the above-mentioned statement and indicates that al-Ḥasan Ibn al-Naḍar, the scribe of the manuscript had copied at Qūṣ up to the folio mentioned in the end of the month of *Rabi'* 1 in the year 547/1152 and had collated the text with the original written by Abu'l-Ḥasan 'Alī Ibn 'Abdu'l-'Azīz Ibn al-'Imām.

The Berlin manuscript, as it is evident from Ahlwardt's *Catalogue*, Vol. IV, No. 5060, was written in J. 670/1271. But its importance lies in the fact that it contained in addition Ibn Bājjah's writings on medicine, Astronomy, and discourses of Alexander of Aphrodisias on sight and colour which are not included in the Bodleian manuscript. As stated by Ahlwardt this manuscript was also based on the copy of Ibn al-'Imām. But the list of the contents shows that the Berlin manuscript was fuller than the Oxford manuscript, and that it lacked only in the logical portion.

The *Kitāb al-Nafs*, in the Bodleian manuscript, consists of 26 folios and a half, beginning at Fol. 138B and ending in Fol. 165A. The manuscript is slightly damaged and, though written in beautiful ***naskh***, is unpointed and often without diacritical marks, as it happens in philosophical manuscripts. Besides the peculiar style of the handwriting, often the letters ا, ک and ل are confusing, which, in the case of orthographic mistakes, have, indeed, rendered the manuscript hardly legible.[33]

However, by collating the *Kitāb al-Nabāt*, in full, the *Risālat al-Wadā'* and the *Risālat Ittiṣāl al-'Aql*, in parts—which were edited by late Professor Asin Palacios from both the Oxford and the Berlin manuscripts[34]—with the corresponding portions available in the Oxford manuscript it is certain that as far as the text of *Kitāb al-Nafs* is concerned the Berlin manuscript would have been of immense help for the editor inasmuch as the two manuscripts sometimes differ from each other in the version of the text, and where one manuscript omits certain words the other manuscript adds certain others.[35] I must also say that in many places in the above-mentioned texts my readings have been different from the readings of the late Professor[36] whose notice certain words have also escaped.[37] His edition of the *Tadbīr al-Mutawaḥḥid* is, however, better than the few pages of the same book published by Mr. D.M. Dunlop who, for example, reads تشكيك as تشكيل, "مشككه as "مشكله, الموهن as الموهين, ردف as رؤف، لهذين as لهتين

and ولذلک لایردف الجمهور as ولذلک لایرد، والجمهور and الامور الجزئیه as "الامور العربیه".[38]

The text obviously contains errors either due to the scribe or due to mistakes in the original copy of Ibn al-'Imām. Most of the errors have been corrected in the text, and the manuscript version has been given in the critical apparatus ; additional words have been bracketed in the text like this (. . .). There are a few lacunas here and there, and I have tried to fill them where possible ; some lacunas may have escaped my notice.

As I said before, the manuscript is very old and in some places the surface of the paper is badly damaged, having been exposed to moisture which caused many pages to stick together. In places the script has been partially or totally covered up by the portions that came off the corresponding portions of the pages facing them.

These damaged parts have been carefully restored, and that with the help of the context and the traces of the original words which can be found. These sections have been placed in between square brackets like this [. . .].

Except *Kitāb Tadbīr al-Mutawaḥḥid*, *Kitāb al-Nabāt*, the *Risālat al-Wadā'* and the *Risālat al-Ittiṣāl*, no other part of this manuscript has ever been edited or published. Ockley's statement in his English translation of Ibn Ṭufayl's *Hayy Ibn Yaqzān* that the whole manuscript of Ibn Bājjah was edited by Professor E. Pocock is highly misleading.[39] Professor Pocock never edited any part of the manuscript nor does he anywhere in the *Elenchos Scriptorum* published along with his *Philosophus Autodidactus*[40] claim to have done it.

FROM IBN BAJJAH'S SAYINGS

Concerning the Soul

CHAPTER I

ON THE SOUL

In the name of Allah, the Merciful, the All-Merciful.
Allah alone helps and directs to the right course.

BODIES are either natural or artificial.[1] Artificial bodies, for example, chair and couch, exist as the result of voluntary action only.[2] Natural bodies, for example, stone, palm-tree, and horse, all come to be and pass away.[3]

Aristotle has explained in his works about the things which are common[4] to natural things (i.e. about the general principles of physics) that all these are composed of form and matter[5] just like artificial bodies, and that the condensation[6] of gold has the same relation to e gold, its matter, as the form of the couch to the wood.

Matter, as explained in the first book of Aristotle's Physics (Fol. 139A), is either formless by itself,[7] and what is generated from it is a simple body (i.e. an element); and the simple bodies (i.e. the elements), as explained in other places, are four[8], namely earth, water, air and fire; or matter has a form. With the exception of the four elements matter of this description can only become the matter for any natural body[9] if another matter be mixed with it. For when a simple being (i.e. element) changes, it changes either in its form, and thus another simple being (i.e. element), opposite to it, is generated from it—from water, for example, is generated air and earth—or it can change in its accidental qualities,[10] but this is transformation, not generation. Now, when an element is bent upon[11] producing a compound, it has necessarily to be mixed with more than one. Similarly, some artificial bodies originate from one existent formed thing, since the species of art are accidental qualities of natural bodies, although their substratum receives them from the artisan[12] only. Some artificial bodies receive the accidental qualities by means that all come from art exclusively, for example, the chair; for its wood receives form through art, and the instruments by which it is made are products of art as well. But there are other artificial bodies in the case of which the first mover is art,[13] while the instruments are natural bodies, as for example, glass which is only finished through the heat of fire, fire being a natural body. This latter kind can be sub-divided: either all the instruments are things which do not exist as a result of voluntary action, or the instruments are in part natural, in part artificial. But how do those things that have natural instruments become artificial ?

I answer : The mover is either accidental or essential,[14] for it may set in motion by itself, or it may set in motion through the intermediary of one or more other things, and these intermediaries are instruments or quasi-instruments for the mover. But the art does not set in motion by itself, but sets in motion through instruments.[15] That which is set in motion in such a way through a mover has more than one mover and will have a last mover and this is the one that is in contact with the thing moved,[16] for example, the axe with the wood, and this is the mover from whom the art derives or who is the art itself.[17] And as has been shown, the last mover cannot set in motion without the first, whereas the first can set in motion without the last, for the motion comes to be at the precise time when the first mover originates movement. Hence, the first mover is the agent for the motion and to him it is ascribed,[18] as has been shown in Physics VIII.

Everything moved in which the first mover is nature is natural, and everything in which the first mover is art is artificial,[19] whatever be its instruments.

As for the fact that the art may change, this is due to an accident or second intention, this has been explained in Physics II.[20]

(Fol. 139-B) Forms, of whatever shape they are, are either natural or artificial.[21] The forms are, in short, the perfections[22] of the bodies in which they are. They are not mere perfections, but perfections firmly established in the bodies like permanent acquisitions. When perfection reaches this state it is called an " entelechy ". Forms are then the entelechies of bodies that possess entelechies potentially. These entelechies are of different kinds :[23] those that perform their actions in the things to which they belong without being moved essentially, and those that perform their actions while being acted upon.

Since everything moved has a mover,[24] the entelechies are moved either by a mover outside them, like most of the artificial bodies, or by a mover inside themselves. In art this is like the automatic machines[25] that are set in motion to perform their actions that remain in them for some time. I have summarized this in the science of Politics.[26]

As to natural bodies, they have their mover inside the whole body, and the natural body is composed of mover and moved.[27] Artificial bodies have their mover outside the thing moved, and the thing moved is connected with the mover by accident.

Natural bodies are, however, not like this. As to the question whether there is in nature anything similar to art, this demands an inquiry, although if there is, this resemblance would seem to be of a different kind.

Natural bodies move to their natural places[28] only when they are in places not natural to them, for, then, there exists in them a capacity[29] according to nature and therefore they have their movements to their places. They only change their directions[30] by accident. For their not being in their natural places is only due to an obstacle that prevents them, but when the obstacle is removed, they move to their natural places. Hence, it has been assumed that the mover in natural bodies is the same as the moved. But this is not so.[31] For in so far as the stone is in potentiality is below and moves inasmuch as it has weight, the thing moved in it is its potentiality of moving downwards, and the mover is the weight.[32] Hence, it moves with one kind of movement that is natural for it.

There is nothing in the thing moved in opposition to the mover, for the thing moved is only its potentiality. This is not the case with those bodies that possess souls.[33] For the thing moved possesses a form for the sake of which it performs a certain action, and either the mover moves them in opposition to their natural action, or moves them according to their nature,[34] e.g. raising the hand and jumping, for through it the body is moved and this is a motion upwards, and therefore the soul moves through an instrument,[35] *i.e.* the natural warmth or something like it.

Forms are of two kinds : (i) the entelechy of a natural body in which the mover and the thing moved are not joined essentially. It is moved without an instrument but is moved as a whole. The other (ii), the entelechy of a natural body moved through instruments. The first is called nature *par excellence* the second is called soul.[36]

Soul is then the entelechy of a natural organic body. There (Fol. 104A) is a first[37] and last[38] entelechy. For a geometer, when actually geometrizing, is called geometer according to the last perfection. So when he geometrizes he is in his last perfection. But soul is the first entelechy.[39] Hence, soul is a first entelechy in a natural organic body. And, the existence of a body with soul is life, so every body having a soul is alive.

It is clear that soul is an equivocal word. For our expression " entelechy " is said in an ambiguous[40] sense, similarly our expression " body " and " instrument ". Soul then is said in a similar ambiguous sense as "weak", " many" and the like. Hence, it is necessary to specify it and so it is said : the nutritive soul is the entelechy of the nutrient organic body, the sensitive the entelechy of the sensitive organic body, the imaginative the entelechy of the imaginative organic body. Soul is, however, predicated of the reasoning soul in a sense though equivocal but more manifest than all these.

All knowledge, as Aristotle says, is noble and beautiful.[41] But some knowledge is nobler than others, and I have already enumerated the grades of sciences in their nobility in many places. The knowledge of the soul (*i.e.* psychology) precedes all sciences, physical and mathematical, with all the kinds of dignity. Again, every science depends upon the science of the soul,[42] because we cannot apprehend the principles of other sciences unless we apprehend soul and know what it is by its definition, as shown in other places. Again, it is a generally admitted fact that one who is not trusted in his knowledge of the state of his own soul is even less fit to be trusted in his knowledge of others. If then we do not know the state and the nature of our soul and if it has not become clear to us whether what has been said about it, has been said correctly or cannot be relied upon, we are even less fit to rely on what appears to us in all other things.

The knowledge of the soul precedes all sciences also because, it gives the enquirer a capacity to grasp those premises without which the physical science cannot be complete. Moreover, political science cannot be treated in an orderly fashion before one knows the nature of the soul.

Again, a science is ennobled either by certainty, that is, when its statements are precise and explicit, or by the nobility and fascination of its subject-matter, as it is the case with the science of the movement of stars (*i.e.* Astronomy). Now, psychology fulfils both conditions. Psychology is worthy of being the most noble science with the exception of the science of the First Principle (*i.e.* Metaphysics). It appears that Metaphysics is different, in an other way, from all other sciences, just as the existents are different from the First Principle. Again, the knowledge of the First Principle is impossible except when it is preceded by the knowledge of the soul[43] and the intellect, otherwise it would be imperfectly known.

The most perfect method of knowing the First Principle is the science in which the capacity provided by psychology is used.

Knowledge of a thing has several kinds of relation;[44] the first and the most deserving of priority is the knowledge of what it is ; the second, the knowledge of its particular essential qualities ; and the third (Fol. 104B), the knowledge of its general essential qualities, is knowledge only in a metaphorical sense.

The knowledge of the quiddity of a thing[45] is either imperfect, *i.e.* known through only one of the complete parts of its definition[46]—this is of various kinds, and the explanation of its kinds has been given elsewhere—or it is perfect, *i.e.* known through what its definition indicates.

Definition *per prius et posterius* is said of meanings all of which are equivocal in their existence and are equally predicated of an object ; definition, therefore, indicates a particular quality of the thing. The expression *per posterius* is used because of the posteriority of everything that is composed of elements which do not constitute the thing, it has been explained elsewhere that the things which constitute a thing are its causes.[47] The definition *per posterius* are not composed of causes, but are only composed[48] of qualities, either far or near,[49] essential or not essential.

The definition *per prius* is that which is composed of causes, and this has also many genera, some of which are composed of farther, some of nearer causes. This (*i.e.* the definition *per prius*) is a definition in a stricter sense.

Causes, in short, are four,[50] matter, agent (*i.e.* efficient cause), form, and end (*i.e.* final cause). They are sometimes particular, sometimes general, that is although specified in form yet general. The most apt to become a definition *per prius* is a definition that consists of the particular cause.[51] Similarly, the causes are sometimes potential and sometimes actual; and the most apt for the definition *per prius* is then the one that consists of the actual particular cause.

This type of definition is either self-evident and thus axiomatic, or derived and found out either by division or by composition, as shown elsewhere.[52] Definitions like these are in the same category as axiomatic definitions,[53] or they are found out by absolute demonstration, and this in three ways:[54] (i) as the conclusion of a demonstration, (ii) as the principle of a demonstration, or (iii) a demonstration with a different arrangement of the terms.[55] This is the most perfect definition and the most deserving of priority.

Signs[56] provide the parts of the definition by accident, not essentially. All this is summarized in the *Posterior Analytics*.

Since we are trying to investigate this kind of knowledge concerning the soul (*i.e.* its definition), how natural it is that its attainment is difficult, but although difficult not impossible.

It is clear that the definition of the soul is not an axiomatic definition, but a derived one.

Again, among the kinds of knowledge that follow, in the first instance, is the knowledge of what the thing[57] is and they are as it were a supplementation of this, which is to know whether the thing is one or not one. If one, whether it consists of parts or not, if it does not consist of parts whether it has several faculties or only one faculty—all this needs investigation in psychology.[58] For all these are views of those who preceded (Aristotle). For some of those who preceded him believed that "soul" indicates plurality, as analogous words do. Others, like Democritus[59] and those who believed in atoms (Fol. 141A), held that it had many parts separately. Yet others like Galen,[60] the physician, held that the soul is one but has many parts in its substrata. This is a view which Plato had already recorded in the *Timaeus*.[61]

A similar question is asked about "soul" in particular, and its solution is so much desired at the very start that it would seem that psychology is only studied for its sake. Namely, the question whether the soul is separable or not at all separable. Hence, you find that Aristotle says at the very beginning of book One[62] that, if there exists a particular action of the soul which distinguishes it from the body, it may be separable. He starts with this topic before beginning the main investigation, because of the aforementioned desire. All this adds to the difficulty of this part of natural science.

Since we are determined[63] on this question, we have to ask whether it belongs to the study of the bodies in which the soul is, or whether it belongs to the qualities which are ascribed to the body in which the soul is, like health and illness, or to the actions which are ascribed to the soul, *e.g.* anger and contentment. Now, if the soul is not separable at all, all the actions related to the soul are shared by the body, although some exist because of the soul and some because of or through the body.[64]

As has been shown in the *Posterior Analytics*,[65] no definition can be formed unless the genus by which it is described is found, for, when we frame a definition which is not composed of the genus of the thing, its parts are indicated by derived words. For of all things that can be predicated of a thing only the genus can be indicated by primary symbol (*i.e.* non-derived word); this definition would express the existence of a thing in a substratum by which it is not explained, so that it would be incomplete and would indicate an imperfection. Hence, we have first to investigate the genus which is to be predicated of the soul and by which it is described, in order to find a way to define the soul. Now, genus and differentia have different aspects, for, the genus is potentially the differentia by receiving its form through the differentia. So potentially it resembles, in a way, the potency which is predicated of matter.[66] Hence, potentially, genus is a thing extraneous to it (*i.e.* the differentia).

Now, the differentia is potentially the definition, just as the whole is said to contain potentially its parts, and the genus exists within the differentia potentially in a manner analogous to the existence of the parts in the whole. This is because when each—genus and differentia-is taken as designating the concrete whole, then the one is genus in so far as it is genus and the other is differentia in so far as it is differentia; but when they are taken in so far as they are definitions, then the genus is the conclusion of a demonstration and the differentia the principle of a demonstration or they both are something analogous. And, therefore, in so far as they are parts of the thing defined, each of them is then potentially the definition but in a different way, as stated (Fol. 141B) in the *Metaphysics*.[67]

Since, as explained in the *Posterior Analytics*,[68] there are three methods for the derivation of the definition :

(i) the method of division, (ii) the method of composition, and (iii) the method in which syllogism is employed, we must ask which method must be followed to define the soul. For this the method of division will not do,[69] for the genus under which the soul is subsumed is unknown, and if it were self-evident the question whether it is a body or not would not arise.

Nor can we follow the method in which syllogism is employed, for the representations in which the soul presents itself are not one, and some of them are composed of things which do not belong essentially together, nor are they necessary deductions from syllogisms, so that it would be possible for us to consider and use the most strong of them. In short, there is no way for us to establish a priority of some to others. Again, when we observe the classes in which the ancient philosophers divided these representations, we will find them neither contradicting nor consistent, but it would seem clear to him who observes them that the term soul is predicated equivocally. Now, if it is possible to understand the representations of the soul, and we are asked for a proof that this is so, if there were any proof, then indeed we find only one among many definitions of which the soul is predicated, but not the real notions of which soul is predicated. For, if soul is predicated equivocally, it is certainly predicated in an ambiguous way. Therefore, only the method of composition remains.

Now, it is evident that the method of composition can only be used for something whose existence is previously known, and the soul is one of the things whose existence is evident ; and to ask for an explanation of its existence is like asking for a proof for the existence of nature. Such a question can only be asked by someone who does not know the difference between self-evident knowledge and the knowledge through something else. Since some known things are self-evident, *e.g.* " horse and man possess soul", but this type of thought can only become coherent[70] through considering all that of which soul is predicated, he (Aristotle), therefore, studies the souls of all the animals ; for, about the forms of plants, there is still scope for investigation.

Now, this kind of study was never undertaken by those who preceded Aristotle.[71] The only aim of the previous philosophers was to consider the human soul in particular to the extent that was necessary for their studying political affairs to which their investigation was, at that time, confined, whereas the various kinds of souls are studied not only for this purpose alone,[72] but because the science of every soul is a part of natural science.

We, therefore, say : every species of animal is a body composed of parts unlike to each other[73] and not connected, but its parts are separate according to their particular ends, and meet together either by coalescence or at a joint ; and this takes place when one of the two is set in motion by the other, for, it is common to all animals. Again, it is (Fol. 142A) a well-known fact that every animal capable of motion, possesses senses: it perceives through parts that move and perceive. It is, therefore, composed of the two (*i.e.* movement and perception).

It is evident that the animal is a genus of body and form, but as to the question in what respect it is said to be composed of body and form, and whether the soul is body or form, this becomes clear to him who relies on the study of his own soul. In his book on the soul,[74] Alexander has discussed about this clearly, so it may be learnt from there.

It is, therefore, established that the soul,[75] as shown before, is a form of the like of this body; and when we use the method of division which we have summarized this implication must be accepted—namely, that the soul is the entelechy of a natural organic body[76]—since it includes every soul and everyone of its faculties, no matter whether it possesses certain particular faculties or certain others.

Since our word " entelechy " is said ambiguously and our expression " natural organic " is not a synonym, like our expression about a dog as " barking dog ",[77] it is clear that soul is said in an ambiguous sense,[78] and that it is an equivocal term.

It is also clear that there is no one nature which comprises all souls,[79] for if the soul were homogeneous, its actions would certainly be homogeneous, whereas no two actions of an animal, like nutrition, sense-perception, locomotion, imagination and reasoning, are homogeneous so that the corresponding faculties of all these actions, too, are not homogeneous ; but some actions precede others, *e.g.* nutrition and sense-perception, and some are similar to each other, *e.g.* sense-perception and imagination. Similarly, the faculties and the soul are in a relation of priority, posteriority and symmetry. Hence, it is impossible to include in the definition of the soul all that is called soul in one and the same way ; hence, the method of demonstration cannot be used in the case of the definition of the soul.

Neglect of this study is one of the reasons due to

which the right treatment of soul escaped the philosophers previous to Aristotle. For they all agreed that soul is a substance,[80] and, therefore, they wanted to subsume it under the species of substance, some saying it is fire,[81] and others blood or air.[82] And, yet an other[83] who realised the absurdity of its being a body made efforts to subsume it under another category. In short, all of them gave it a place in the ten categories.

Since, it had become clear to Plato that the soul must be subsumed under substance which is, as explained by him, predicated of the matter which is body, and of the form,[84] and that it is absurd to assume soul as a body, he made efforts to define soul in a way special to it. And, as he postulated that the forms of the spherical bodies are souls, he investigated that which is shared by all of them, and found that sense-perception is the characteristic of the animal,[85] and motion is common to all, he, therefore, defined soul by saying : " It is a thing which moves itself."[86] For the word " thing " indicates here the same as we say " being". Such was his definition of the soul, because Plato believed that every mover is moved, since according to him (Fol. 142B) nothing can cause motion unless it is moved;[87] and this view has been summarized in *Physics VII*.[88]

Concerning the refutation of the views recorded about the soul, Aristotle has explained it thoroughly in the first book of the *De Anima*,[89] so let us assume his conception in general.

Let us now turn to the study of the soul which Aristotle initiates out in the way we shall describe.

Since some souls[90] are *per prius* by nature, and some are *per posterius*, and the last of all in appearance is the imaginative soul. For the sense-perception precedes them. It is sometimes assumed[91] that some animals have no imagination, *e.g.* the worm and the fly,[92] and if they did possess imagination, it is neither separable from sensation nor is it determinate.

The most prior of all the faculties of sensation is the faculty of touch, the faculty of sense-perception being preceded by the faculty of nutrition which is, hence, the most prior of all the faculties of soul.

The reasoning faculty, though itself soul, is the last to appear in nature in the same way as the perfect comes after the imperfect in nature.

Aristotle has,[92] therefore, started with the investigation of the nutritive soul. This kind of the soul has two faculties : (i) one the faculty of growth, and (ii) the other the faculty of generation. The nutritive faculty, thus, precedes all and is, then, the most prior of the faculties of soul.

CHAPTER II

DISCOURSE ON THE NUTRITIVE FACULTY

We say : The opposite of being is not-being. Not-being is either impossible,[1] *i.e.* that which cannot exist, or possible. What is possible is of two kinds : one, the necessary,[2] is that whose non-existence is impossible, and the other, that which just exists, *i.e.* that which exists at a particular time ; so it is clear that that which just exists was non-existing at another particular time. It is sometimes assumed that it entails for its non-existence in an infinite time. But if this is the case, it is so by accident, as has been summarized, in *Physics VIII.*[3] As has been shown there, let it be understood that the non-existence[4] of this is also absolute non-existence. But the absolute non-existence necessarily implies possibility,[5] since necessarily it is an equivocal term. The relation of non-existence to possibility is clear from what we have explained in *Physics I.* Not being is the opposite being in relation to matter in so far as it is essentially an opposite being. By opposite I mean that of which the two contraries, the affirmative and the negative, are composed, *i.e.* whenever the opposite is predicated of one and the same substratum —I mean one thing and its contrary the two statements become contraries, and are distinguished according to being true or false.

When, for instance, we say about Zaid, when he is ill, that he can recover or not, the opposite of "he can recover", which makes up this statement, is not the existence of privation of health which is linked up with its possibility, but it is "the privation of health" at the moment which contains the statement, "he can recover", no matter whether this time is determined or not determined. Hence, the relation of "health" to the substratum—in respect of that which has a like, like this opposite—is the possibility of health. The potentiality, in the relation of health to matter is the non-existence of health, but not in so far as it has an opposite in potentiality. It is the relation of the opposite form to the substratum, but not in so far as it is opposite. Therefore they are mutually interdependent.

The possible and what is potential are one in the substratum but two in expression. Hence, as shown in *Physics VIII*, it necessarily follows that potentiality precedes actuality in time,[6] *e.g.* it is said of the moon, "it can eclipse and it is potentially eclipsable", but in an equivocal sense; potentiality in the moon is nearer to the univocal expression than our expression "possible", because "possible" is equivocally used for both "the moon" and the "ill man", and therefore, "eclipse" has been enumerated among the necessary things.

As explained in many places, potentiality precedes actuality,[7] and actuality is divided into the ten categories.

No potential, however, does become actual before it reaches a state when change becomes necessary, as has been shown in *Physics VIII.*[8]

Change takes place in substance, quantity, quality and space,[9] and it is the faculties of these four through which the thing moved is set in motion. The faculties by which the thing moved is set in motion are called passive and changing faculties, the faculties connected with this process being changing faculties.

There is hardly any category among the remaining categories that is being acted upon, since the entelechy of their passive faculties is not change, but it is due to change, and hence, it takes place at the present time.[10]

This relation, however, is not found in the definition of the three categories. Quantity, for example, is not defined through the relation of the substance, *i.e.* the substratum, to it, nor is quality. But quantity is the most apt for this, so much so that it has been assumed that it can be separated from substratum. All the other six categories are defined through their relation to a substratum. But the categories of Position and Possession have substance in their definitions, whereas the remaining four are different, since their substrata can be something different from substance. All these, however, have this in common that they have substrata, in the definitions of which this relation is not found.

But the categories in which the relation is found in the definition of one of the two substrata, in so far as they are two contradictories, are Position, Possession, Space, Time and Passivity. Those categories in which the relation is not found in the definition of one of them, are of two kinds: either both of the substrata are together in actuality,[11] and this is the category of Relation, or one of the two is actual and the other potential in so far as it is potential, and this is the category of "Being acted upon".

The problem whether there exist two existents in actuality that are substrata for a relationship which is found in the definition of the two and is due to Relation, has been explained elsewhere.

Now, it is obvious that that which acts, in so far as it is that which acts, exists in actuality, and that which is acted upon exists in potentiality, since from our word يفعل (it acts) it follows essentially and not accidentally that it exists in actuality as a fully specified particular, and from ماينفعل (that which is acted upon) it necessarily follows that it exists in potentiality. That which acts accompanies[12] in existence that which is acted upon, and it entails that its being is necessary.

The thing moved has either eternal or transitory movement. The mover of the eternal movement is one and is moving eternally. Hence, the mover of the eternal movement is always one, existent in actuality, and he is not such as to move at one time and not at another That which causes a transitory movement is either one and the same which is at one time moving and at another not, *e.g.* the weight in the stone that moves at one time and does not move at another, or is one after another. Whatever the case, this is a kind of mover. It, therefore, entails on both (whether the mover is one or more than one) that at a certain time they do not move, the more explicit being the former case, *i.e.* the mover being one that moves at a time and does not move at another, as the weight that is hindered by an obstacle, similarly, the souls of the animals prevented from movement, the plant that has not yet started growing, the fire when it finds nothing to burn, and the snow when it finds nothing to cool down. All these, then, do not move, but are capable of moving. As has been shown,[13] that which is possible is potential, and that which can move when it does not actually move is potentiality, and this potentiality characterises the active and the moving faculties. Thus it has been shown what the moving faculties are.

Those faculties that are moved are necessarily in a body,[14] because everything that is moved is divisible,[15] and they are called faculties *per prius.* But the moving faculties are only called faculties *per posterius* and relatively.

It has been shown and summarised in the *Metaphysics* how the moving faculties exist sometimes in bodies either as forms or as accidents,[16] and sometimes do not exist in bodies[17] so that their existence can be shown. As such are enumerated the Active Intellect and the Acquired Intellect.[18]

But the souls of the spherical bodies[19] are not at all and by no means faculties. If they are called faculties it is so in another way; and in relation to the Active Intellect, they are moving faculties, but not in so far as the Active Intellect resembles them but in so far as they resemble the Active Intellect in existence ; and so they are called faculties by way of accidental resemblance. This is a different kind which is called so ambiguously, but this is the ambiguous meaning nearest to the equivocal sense.

Food can be understood as potential, just as "meat" for the wild animal. Food can also be understood of the last food [20] as for example the blood (into which the digested food turns). The faculty of nutrition, then, is a faculty by which the body becomes "moved" being, therefore, a passive faculty.

As everything which changes has a changer, the potential food which is the far food has necessarily a mover that turns it into actual food—its activity being to provide nourishment. The mover is the nutrient, and the body that has a faculty like this is that which is nourished. The forms of the words correspond to the meanings they indicate, since the nutriment is that which is being acted upon, while the perfection of the mover is that it is moving, and the form[21] of its verbal expression is the form of the expression "movement". But why this is so, we shall explain somewhere else.[22]

What takes food is either a plant or an animal, in both of them there is a moving faculty[23]; so the body which takes food has a moving faculty. Every moving faculty is necessarily a perfection. Hence, in the body there is something that exists actually and by which the food is moved.

As it is clear from the investigation about this faculty (*i.e.* the faculty of nutriment), the process of nutrition takes place only through organs. The nutritive faculty then is a soul. Sometimes they doubt about Quantity whether its faculty is a soul or not. If its faculty be a soul, then every soul does not necessarily move by an organ, because Quantity consists of parts alike to each other in sense-perception; even though there is no growth[24] in Quantity by addition to that which is already there, as in the case of the stone. Similarly, objection is raised about the sponge of the sea[25] as to whether it is an animal or a plant. In short, we find that Nature does not change from one genus into a more perfect genus unless it produces an intermediary[26]; but the investigation of this is somewhere else.

As we have said,[27] change occurs in substance and occurs in the rest of the categories. Nourishment takes place only through producing a movement in the substance. This is clear when we investigate food For blood and milk are different from meat, and different from the water mixed with earth which is the food of the plant, as has been described in the book of *Animals and the book of Plants.* [28]

The movement of food is transitory, food being generated and the nutrient generating. Hence, the function of the nutritive faculty is to produce movement in substance. We have thus found the genus[29] under which the nutritive soul is to be subsumed. This faculty is an agent (active), and every agent is actually existing ; and every being that has no other activity has two perfections:[30] a first perfection which is its existence in potentiality, and a last perfection which is its existence in motion. Now, the nutritive soul is the first entelechy of the nourished. But as to the nature of its generations[31]—and, this is the definition which is called the principle of demonstration—this will be clear from what I say :

Food is either potential, or actual,[32] and that which is potential is either far, as the elements,[33] or near, as meat and vegetables for the animal, while the near nutriment for the plant has no name. The far is that in which the mover is not the nutritive faculty, and the near is that what is moved by the nutritive faculty. This latter (*i e* the near one) has again grades : (i) the food that reaches the organs of nourishment in the animal, and the moisture that exists in the roots of the plant, (ii) the food that is nearer than these, for example, the blood[34] that runs in veins and the milk (*i.e.* sap) in the plant as long as it is tender, and (iii) the last perfection, for example, the blood that turns into flesh, and the sap that changes into fibre and so it is acquired by the fibre.

And as everything that is opposite to that what is potential is opposite to that what is actual, we say :[35] He who holds that food is derived from المضاد (that which nourishes) does not contradict the view of the one who holds that all food is from the like. For the first proceeds from that which is food potentially and the second from that which is food actually, and food is said of both equivocally—this rejects the doubt that arises concerning food.

As to which particular species of generation produces food and how it generates, all these will be made clear by what we say :

We say : Every being that comes to be and passes away has an activity peculiar to it and for the sake of which it comes to be, as has been shown somewhere else. And, through this particular activity it has become a part of the universe, because nature has done nothing in vain.

As every generation has a generator, the generator either belongs to the species of the one that comes into being or to its genus.[36] The thing generated is either artificial—its generator then being art which exists in a way different from the product of art, but art is in various matters—or natural, the generator of the natural product being natural. In short, the thing moved sometimes belongs to the species of the mover and sometimes not; for fire comes from fire, heat from heat, but hard is caused either by cold or by hot.

Hence, the faculties of the physical bodies are either movers or not so.[37]

The moving faculty then performs essentially and primarily those actions which belong to their species, and secondarily and accidentally something else and that according to the matters in which they act. Every moving faculty, besides the fact that it has its peculiar kind of existence, has an " intention " by which it produces its like[38]. Among the elements this potentiality is evident in fire, next in air, and the least evident in water and earth. But the like of this potentiality only imparts natural forms to the bodies having parts alike to each other. But fire is sometimes produced by something else, as it is produced by striking the fire-stone.

All animate bodies have a generative faculty, which, in short, is the faculty which generates from the food potentially a body which is similar to the body in which it is.[39] So necessarily this animate body, in the peculiar existence of the faculty, becomes an "intention" by which the faculty moves towards the existence that characterises it. This generative faculty is both ruling in that body, being in a part of the faculty which is the principle of that body, as for example, the heart in the animal,[40] and a serving and particular being in every organ of the body. The form of the bone in the body, for example, is a potentiality that stirs the food, which is a bone potentially, to become an actual bone. The case is similar with regard to flesh and the rest. That which is in the ' beginning ' comes into being from the food that is in the being This has been summarised elsewhere.[41]

It is clear that a body that has such a form is composed of the elements, and that it is composed oı earth and water. As shown before,[42] the composed is mixed primarily only when its ingredients are moved in space. Then they come near[43] to each other, and next each part is transformed into another in the way shown in the first book of *De Generatione et Corruptione*. But this (*i.e.* transformation) is not possible through cold and is possible only through heat. This heat is the organ of the scul and is called the innate animate heat, as has been explained in the seventeenth section of *the book of Animals*.[44]

The innate heat is, therefore, the organ of this soul. Then, the nutritive soul first moves the innate heat, which is moved by itself, and moves through innate heat the food. For that which is not moved cannot move what is not in it except by moving it first through a body that is in it, as has been shown in *Physics* VIII.[45]

This faculty (*i.e.* the nutritive faculty) causes a movement like this, and changes what is potentially an "intention" in it to be actually like it.[46]

Since all that contains moisture is speedily acted upon and dissolved, the body of everything which has soul is like it.[47] And, hence, if it is bent upon to preserve that body, it must possess a faculty like this, because if a body is left without a substitute for that portion of it which is dissolved, the body is sure to perish.[48]

All natural body has a particular kind of size by which its being is completed, as it is evident in many plants and animals. It is not provided with that size from the very beginning of its generation, since then the body did not yet possess a faculty through which it could be moved to that kind of size. This faculty is the soul of growth.[49] Hence the nutritive soul prepares more food than what is dissolved so that it does not only become a substitute in the part of the body for what is dissolved but also a surplus,[50] and then that body is moved and gains a kind of size which it did not possess before.

This "movement" evidently has no name which comprehends it as well as the name of the movement of growth and the name of the movement of increase, and their two opposites, the movement of decay and diminishing. I have explained this "movement" in the first book of *De Generatione et Corruptione*.[51]

Now, this is another faculty which is in the first nutritive faculty like the form, the first faculty being for it like matter, because the faculty of growth cannot dispense with the nutritive faculty,[52] and hence, when the body reaches its natural perfection, the nutritive faculty produces less food, but in a quantity sufficient to substitute what is dissolved from the body. This is the function of these two kinds of soul.

Every body that takes nourishment is either reproductive or not reproductive. The reproductive body, in short, is that body whose form possesses a faculty which moves what belongs in potentiality to that species and turns it into that species in actuality.

The difference between this reproductive façulty and the nutritive faculty is this : the nutritive faculty turns each of those parts which potentially exist, actually into its parts, while the reproductive faculty turns what is potentially that species into a body of that species without employing the parts of the nutritive faculty in it, as has been explained in the sixteenth book of the *book of Animals*.[53]

This reproductive faculty is related to the body reproduced just as the art is related to the chair, because the reproductive faculty, as explained in that book, is in a matter different from that of the reproduced in the same way as it happens in the art.

This faculty (*i.e.* the reproductive) is not in a body but it is *mind in actuality*,[54] as has been shown in that book. But the nutritive faculty is a faculty in a body, since it is material. Hence, when the reproductive faculty acts upon matter suitable for it and makes it generate the same species in it, that form (*i.e.* the reproductive) causes this kind of movement[55] (*i.e.* reproduction). Thus it is clear that the action of the generative faculty is not through the nutritive faculty, but is something else.[56]

It is also clear that the faculty we described as reproductive of the species does not reproduce something like itself in the same way as we say of a substratum that it is like the art.[57] As shown before, this faculty is always found connected with a certain body in order to move that which it has to move, namely, that which is potentially moveable.

The body whose form is like this is sometimes found in air and in water, and the generation of such beings is caused by different movers, *e.g.* the putridity in animals out of which they are generated.[58] These are bodies that are not reproductive but they are provided with nothing more than their mere existence. Their species, therefore, needs another species for the preservation of its existence. But the species of the animate and reproductive bodies are provided besides their existence with a capacity that provides them with a continuation of their existence. For succession[59] is in the nature of continuation, and since it has a connection it is a being.[60] This is the most imperfect stage of the necessary existence.

But the continuation of the species that are not reproductive is the arrangement of the periods of their existence. This is the lowest rank of the necessary existence. The reproductive species then is in the middle between the noblest rank of existence, namely, the absolutely necessary existence, and the lowest rank of existence in which the meaning of necessary existence is " arrangement ".

Since material bodies have no necessary existence, they have been given reproduction in exchange for it.

Reproduction takes place through a faculty by which it moves the food until some of it becomes a body that has a faculty like this, I mean the faculty of reproduction, and it has already been said[61] what the nature of this body is. It is called sperm in those animals that have sperm, as has been demonstrated in the *book of Animals.*[62]

Thus this faculty (of reproduction) is like the form for that (*i.e.* the faculty of growth), and as though it were the extreme [63] of the movement of the faculty of growth, and hence, it acts only when it reaches the perfection of its movement. The nutritive faculty is like matter for the reproductive faculty and the faculty of growth is like immediate antecedent. And this (*i.e.* the reproductive faculty) is like the end; and we do not find for the nutritive soul any faculty more perfect than this.

It is clear that the nutritive faculty always produces in such bodies more nutrition than is required for the preservation of the body, and that this surplus [64] is first spent in growth, and when the body is mature, sperm developes from it. As the sperm is the surplus of the last food, hence, the faculty of reproduction does not cease except in old age,[65] when the nutritive faculty restricts its activity to the preservation of the body only, the nutritive faculty is then singled out from the growing faculty and exists exclusively alone.

Hence, it has been shown what the nutritive soul is, why it is and which are its organs; and that the soul and all its faculties are in one substratum, no matter whether it is a single part or a part that comes to be in succession in it, as we find in many plants and in some animals.

CHAPTER III

DISCOURSE ON THE FACULTIES OF SENSE-PERCEPTION

Every body, as shown elsewhere,[1] is composed of form and matter, both being incorporeal[2] while the body exists through both of them.[3] Matter, in so far as it is matter, does not essentially[4] possess a form, but it receives form. In a body form does not actually exist separated from matter, nor matter in it actually separeted from form.[5] But in a body composed of the two each can be potentially separated from the other. This is evident in the transitory bodies.

But, body, matter and form are predicated of the spherical bodies and of the bodies that come to be and pass away equivocally,[6] as has been shown elsewhere. As shown in *Physics I*, an organic[7] matter is sometimes separated from form, as becomes manifest at the moment of decay[8]. It is thus clear that the fully specified particular is neither actually distinct nor changeable in any way of change. Change only occurs when the fully specified particular is moved to come into existence or to cease to be.

Matter does not at all exist separately from form, but it is separated only to be connected with another form[9] ; and then the absence of form is manifest in it. It necessarily follows from this that the form by itself is also separable from matter either to be connected with another matter or to have existence by itself, since, otherwise, it is not possible that matter is somehow different from form and form from matter, and change would be meaningless, and there would necessarily follow from it other absurdities, *e.g.* generation and corruption, and "motion"[10], in general, will be meaningless; to assume the existence of a mover belonging to the species of the thing moved, will also be absurd. Again, just as the matter of water, when it disappears and turns into vapour, exists in connection with the form of vapour, not so that the form of vapour becomes its specific form, but so that the form of vapour is continuously connected with the matter of water. Form then has either matter, not so that it is a matter for the form through which the form becomes a form—just as matter is represented by the form, when it is that particular specified body[11]—but so that as it exists by nature it is in a substratum without having any possibility of existence in itself, since it is an "immattered" form; or form possesses matter in a way suitable to the existence of matter with form. For whenever matter receives form it becomes the substratum for the form, being in itself formless matter. Hence, there are in matter forms which are potentially opposed to each other. So, this potentiality is a necessary corollary of the matter and is not separable from it.

Hence, if it is possible that a form exists which has no opposite, for the matter with which the form is connected is only a substratum,[12] it is matter only in an equivocal sense of the term, since matter has essentially no relation with any particular form; but all forms are related to it equally. This is because everything moved has a mover, for example, the pieces of woods in art which are not at all without form; and when whichever particular form is determined in matter it remains all the while capable of receiving the contrary form. When the form comes to it, it sets it into motion.[13]

A mover is of two kinds:[14] either not-homogeneous as the mover of the spherical bodies which moves them by necessity, or homogeneous. This second mover, then, has matter which is again capable of receiving a form opposite to the first. Let AB, for example, be water. Now, in AB there is the form of the water, and let that be coolness, since it contains coolness in actuality which is air in potentiality. So, let there be H for the potentiality of air. Now, in AB there are B and H. Hence, AB causes motion in so for as it is B, and suffers motion in so far as it is H. That which opposes (*i.e.* the opposite form supposed to be received by matter in potentiality) is A which has J, then in AJ there is J which is its form and it contains M, that is its being that which is potential; and what is potential cannot be moved without a mover. The bodies of AB and AJ, therefore, are at rest in so far as they are H and M, and movers in so far as they are B and J. Hence, the capacity of H is necessarily moved by J, and the capacity of M by B. If B is equal to J then it will not be moved, nor will either of the two. If on the contrary, one of the two is stronger, and let B, for instance, necessarily, move AM, the matter being B and its substratum, then, there will necessarily follow H, because BJ are homogeneous and contraries But this is not the case with that in which forms are not contraries For example, "This thing is wood, and a chair potentially". Now the thing may be a chair while it is wood as it was so before, because the chair is not homogeneous to the wood in the same sense as "hot" is to "cold", nor does the existence of the potentiality of the chair in the wood essentially belong to the wood, nor is the wood the cause of the existence of the potentiality in the wood except in a different way.

As concerning "hot" and "the potentiality of cold", the fact that it is hot is the cause of its being potentially cold,[15] and therefore "hot" is potentially "cold" since "hot" and "cold" are related to matter in the same way.[16] Hence, matter receives "hot", in the way as it receives "cold", these two being different from each other. If matter were to receive the two together, then surely there would remain no difference at all. They are different from each other only because the matter belonging to both of them accepts "straightness", and the "straight" is the first cause of contrariety,[17] since the "straight" brings about perfection, but is not perfect in itsef. It has, therefore, a middle and two extremes,[18] because it is continuous, and everything that is "continuous" consists of parts[19]—but this discourse is suitable for the study of the cause of the existence of contraries—and the faculty that is moved and belongs to it (*i.e.* the continuous) has nothing to make it "more" or "less"[20] except that it is in a larger or smaller body. A body is larger or smaller in so far as it is actually that specific body, because it is due to its quiddity that the existing size belongs to it by nature. "The less" and "the more" exist for two contraries only in so far as they actually exist. Moreover, "the more" and "the less" are called by way of analogy. Hence, it follows necessarily, when the matter of the contraries is one, that one acts and the other is acted upon. But when the matter is not one, then neither of the two is acted upon by the other, but the moved is set into motion and the mover causes motion.

Matter is either near or far. Now, the contraries whose near matter is one in species are like air and water ; but those whose far matter is one in species and whose near matter varies in species are like the artisan and the wood in the case of the chair ; and hence, no artisan can be greater than the other in the case of the one and the same wood.

Since the far matter is common to mover and moved, sometimes the wood moves the artisan as e.g. the fatigue that overtakes him;[21] and in this case the matter is far. For everything that sets something into motion, while the matter of the mover and the moved is different, not at all common, does not procure fatigue to the mover, but since the mover possesses matter, it follows necessarily that the mover has a relation with the moved.[22] This is the case, for example, with the spherical bodies and the elements. But if the mover has no matter, then that mover moves without fatigue, and without any relation in quantity to the thing moved, because it has no parts. And if the mover is not sufficient by itself, then its movement will have a relation to the one that assists him. If it is possible, the mover moves sometimes and does not move some other time, like "intellect", or it causes different movement, as it happens in most intermediate things.

If the mover is sufficient to cause motion by itself, then it necessarily moves eternally and with an eternal uniform movement, like the Prime Mover.

Matter, then, in every body necessarily requires

for its existence to be dressed with a form either near or far. The fact about matter, as Plato[23] says, is that due to its need and ugliness matter avoids manifesting itself, and so it conceals itself as it were in any possible form.[24] And these states accompany matter when it is separated from form. Let us see then what happens to form when it is abstracted, and how this happens.

The principle applicable to this is that when an individual specified body exists one points to it, because the form and the matter of this body have not at all any discrepancy[25] between themselves in any way, whether potentially or actually. Hence, both of them are a single thing,[26] that is, "this specified individual".

Everything is due to a certain inclination,[27] and hence, when a thing exists separately from an other thing, the other in its turn inclines to be separable from it.

But the question how two things which are actually not at all different from each other are potentially different is the same as the existence of the part in a continuous whole whose parts are all alike. For two parts in this whole are actually one but potentially different. Difference only arises, on the one hand, due to form, and on the other, due to matter. But how form and matter become one thing actually while being different potentially, potentiality being always only the matter, has been demonstrated in the *Metaphysics*.[28] Here, potentiality indicates something different from what is indicated by our expression بالقوة (in potentiality)[29] in change, because the being of form here is not potentially different from matter in so far as when one of the two is changed the "aggregate" is decomposed, but in a different way.[30] For the form that characterises this "aggregate" decays necessarily when the "aggregate" decays; and the matter assumes an other form,[31] and through this reshaping there arises another aggregate. But the relation of the (second) form to the species of the first form exists in this process in the matter,[32] and thus, through this relation the matter imitates that which is actual,[33] as has been shown elsewhere.

But form cannot be set in motion[34] in the same way as matter, so as to become different; but it is different by necessity. How can the form, then, be different? That form is not moved essentially is evident, because it is not divisible;[35] that it is moved by accident is not impossible, as has been shown in the *Physics*.[36] But, how does form become through its accidental movement something, while the movement is accidental; and how does this state happen to form so as to become through it a different entity?

We reply: It is an agreed fact that nature does not do anything in vain, nor is there in the universe anything without a purpose at all. And, every existent comes to be either for the sake of something else or for the sake of itself.[37] The aim of that which exists for the sake of something else is to be connected with that for the sake of which it exists.

Connection is either in existence, like the connection of the soul with body, and the connection of that which suffers change with that which causes change—no matter whether the connection is by change, or by being acted upon, or by habit and the like—or it is the connection of matter, namely, the connection of a body with a body. This is of various kinds: first, the connection of the body with that which contains it, namely, connection in space, second, the connection of the moving body with the body that is moved. As shown in *Physics VII*,[38] the most prior of all these connections is the connection in space, since all that is changed has somthing to cause change.

Connection is said of the connection of being[39] and the connection of body *per prius et posterius.* Connection in space is essentially the connection of a body with a body. The rest of the kind is the connection of a body with a body by accident.

It is clear that everything is either a body or in a body, or not at all a body nor in a body. I mean by my expression " in a body " all that which needs for its existence a body, for it has been demonstrated that there is an existent which does not need, for its existence, a body, and that on the contrary, the body needs it for its existence, and that it is connected with the body in this way, as has been explained at the end of *Physics VIII*, and in the sixteenth book of the book of *Animals.*[40] New, "this" (" incorporeal being ") is neither a body nor is in a body; it cannot have any connection except in existence alone. Hence, if there is a thing that exists for the sake of something else, and this something, for the sake of which the thing has come into being, is a body, then it is necessary that the former is connected with the latter corporeally, although the latter does not owe its existence to the former so that the latter be in the former, as health in man. "This" is then necessarily a body, because if it were not a body then there would be no connection between the former and the latter at all.

The immattered forms do not exist for their own sake, but are for the sake of something else, for nature does not make anything without a purpose. As shown in the book of *Heavens and Earth*,[41] the elements are for the sake of the spherical bodies,[42] because the spherical body is in the elements in the same way as the body is in space; and they are in the spherical body in the same way as a part is in the whole. For the universe is like a single separate animal which requires nothing from outside at all. Hence, the form of the elements, is necessarily in matter. And, since the extreme cause, that is the final cause, is the most excellent being ; hence, its being after the elements must necessarily be in a substratum, because that for the sake of which the elements come to be is so. For, if the spherical body were not necessarily in a substratum then the elements would not need be in a substratum. Hence, the existence of those forms in a substratum is the cause of the being of the elements in a substratum. Thus, the body is said of those (the spherical bodies) and of these (i.e. elements) *per prius et posterius*, and this makes clear what has been doubted by Abū Naṣr in his treatise on "the Intelligence and the Intelligible".[43]

It has been shown that matter, as assumed by Aristotle, exists only for the sake of the existence of form,[44] but for the sake of the last existence of the form and not for the sake of its first existence; and the doubt has arisen only in so far as its first existence is concerned.

Sometimes a doubt is expressed against this view and is said: "The last existence is the best existence, the first existence of form being the most incomplete, and so, the corporeal being is better than the intelligible being. This contradicts what Plato says and what is known of the doctrine of the Peripatetics".

We reply: " Our expression 'the best being' is said in two ways. First, in an absolute sense, then this is clear that the intelligible being is better than the sensible being,[45] because the object of mind is more suited to existence than the object of sense, since the former is the principle of the latter,[46] as has been demonstrated by Plato, Aristotle and many other Peripatetics. And what is the most suited to existence is called the best in existence. Second, a being is sometimes called ' the best ' in relation to different species of existing things, but not so that it is for the sake of that existent. So that the term 'being' which belongs to the existent would not be from the genus of the best, and its best being would only be from the genus of the last perfect being, this best being existing not in so far as it is the species of 'existence', but in so far as something characterises it. It is, therefore, said that the immattered form is intelligible not essentially but in so far as mind has made it.

But, someone may doubt and say: " If it were not inherent in the essence and existence of the being which is a property of the immattered forms that they are intelligible, they would not become intelligible, because everything exists for a purpose and it is in the nature of the thing to receive that purpose, and that which has not in its nature to receive anything, neither near nor far, cannot have anything neither essentially nor accidentally".

We reply: " That it is in the nature of the immattered forms to be somehow intelligible has not been assumed in the argument; and that their being intelligible is in their particular being is not the case. But it is through that of which they are constituted that they receive the intelligible existence, and when they are connected with the mover they obtain that being, hence, they need something else in order to have that being. This something is their connection with the mover which comes to them from outside. Hence, it is not in their essence that they become intelligible, but it is something else which makes them intelligible. Hence, they always; in order to become intelligible, need this connection which makes them entirely accomplished in existence. So the perfection of their being which is peculiar to them would be from the genus of the imperfect being; and when they take their share from the best being they confine themselves to the best being. It is for the sake of this that every (form) tries to be free from matter and is necessarily separable from it, as it is said of the 'Acquired Intellect' ".

But someone may doubt this view and say: "Forms being objects of mind is the same as their being actually unconnected. It, therefore, follows that there is in nature something without a purpose. Hence, the same doubt comes back".

We reply: "These immattered forms are sometimes sensible and imaginable, and are then movers of desire, anger and many other things.[47] They have, therefore, functions which are for them either in respect of their being in their particular matters, and so they are designated by their respective terms; or are in respect of their being sensible and imaginable, and so not designated by those terms. But the genus is called 'a soul' set in motion', and there is no particular name for every particular kind of it."

But someone may ask and say the same thing about their being intelligible (i.e. that which has been just now said about their being sensible and imaginable). Their being intelligible means that some of them do not actually exist at all. But this doubt should only be investigated while considering the existence of the universe and the mutual relations of its parts. For, the being of the intelligible for the sake of something else is different from the being of the material for the sake of something else, the two beings being, indeed, opposite to each other.[49] It is for this reason (i.e. the intelligible being is different from the material being) that Abū Naṣr says: "They become an existent of the universe."[50]

Since the mover acts sometimes and does not act some other time, there must be a change by necessity here. But the mover is not body, and the change is then in the immattered form. And, since all that is not divisible is not changeable, change will happen to the immattered form by accident,[51] that is, through a changeable. So the immattered form necessarily always needs matter in order to be changed through it.[52] This connection is not to be called a change in space, because one of the two (connected) is not body, nor is it near nor far. This connection is, therefore, only in its being.[53]

Hence, for a material thing there are two kinds of change, one preceding the other in the same way as they do in their principles. One is "change in space", its principle being the material being in so far as it is in a substratum. For the material being indicates it (i.e. change) in so far as it is becoming and not in so far as it is an existent. The other change is for the sake of this being that is extraneous to its essence and precedes that other being just as the-movement-in-space precedes the other movements. But the change in quantity, such as growth, is a characteristic of some marterial bodies that take nourishment.

Change-in-being means that "this", for instance, is in a nearer stage in existence.[54] This is because this stage has a certain discrepancy in it. We have already said that this is not possible concerning the immattered forms except for the sake of the mover, while the thing moved cannot cause motion. It is, therefore, clear that existence must be mixed with the elements of which none deserves existence more than the material being and it is mixed with the elements;[55] its movement is sometimes caused by a mover homogeneous to it, as is the case in those animate bodies which are reproductive, and some are moved by the spherical bodies, e.g. the souls of those that are generated but are not reproductive.

Since the discourse is concerning the existence of the immattered forms as separated from matter, namely, the "actual intellect",[56] it is clear that this is the ultimate cause[57] of all that we have said before.

This kind of existence in matter cannot exist actually unless it is in such states as are limited e.g. taking nourishment,[58] and the most able being is the one free in taking suitable food as well as in the rest of that by which alone one's being is accomplished, namely, man.

Now, then, necessarily the faculty of reason precedes the rest of the faculties of the soul in existence, and the rest of the faculties exist for the sake of this faculty which is the best; and hence, the rest of the faculties and imagination are generated for the sake of the reasoning faculty. This[59] is not by necessity, as has been held by those who believe that since the elements get mixed together in equal proportion they cause sensation by chance.

Form, then, has grades. First grade is its existence in matter,[60] and there is not at all any change in it. This is the most extreme one, the other extreme being its opposite, namely, its being intelligible. This is the most extreme side. But, for being intelligible, it requires a material being of which it is constituted. For that is the principle of its existence. Perfection is of all principles the most deserving to be a principle, and so it is not at all possible for this form to be separated from matter. Whenever it is separated it is a wrong contrivance. Hence, it follows necessarily that the study of nature must be concerned with "the forms with matter". This will be explained in the discussion on the faculty of reason[61] which is never without a substratum, since it is made so in its nature. When form is found to be different it is evident that it is connected with a mover in proportion to its difference which depends upon the degree of abstraction. The same applies to every immattered form, I mean, that it exist in its substratum in the sense that the substratum is its matter. Thus, form and the elements are in one and the same grade. But when form exists somehow separated from matter whether by being abstract or by having a substratum—the state of its substratum in relation to being however is not like the state of matter in relation to form—then however it may be, it is called perception.

But the abstraction of the immattered form is not possible, because, as shown before,[62] its relation to matter is in itself. Hence, necessarily there is, in the bodies possessing form, an "intention" by which the form is connected with the matter. So, as long as it is connected with the matter it is intelligible, and when matter is changed it becomes intelligible potentially.

This separation is of various grades, each grade being called a soul, and a psychical faculty while it is a grade. To these belongs sense-perception, next imagination, next reasoning which is the extreme. As for taking nourishment, what position it possesses, we shall soon explain latter on. We have already discussed for which purpose these grades exist. All these are for the sake of the reasoning faculty.

But that these are grades is self-evident, since sense-perception and imagination are things manifestly existent.

But, which of these grades is sense-perception, and how it comes to be, all these will be clear by when we shall say.

We say: It is evident that sense-perception is actual,[63] like the state of an animal that is awake when it perceives; and sometimes potential, like an animal that sleeps and keeps his eyes closed. Potentiality is either near or far[64]—far like the capacity of sense-perception in the embryo, and near like the sense of small when no object of smell is present, and like the sense of sight in darkness. Similarly, it is generally admitted that no species does perceive anything by any organ[65] at random. Animals, for example, do not see with their month nor taste with their eyes.

All that is potential can only be actual when it is changed by something that causes change, as has been shown in *Physics VIII*.[66]

Thus it is necessary for sense-perception to have an object that suffers change and an agent that causes change[67]. It is clear that the object of movement is different from the mover. The mover is then the object of perception and its being a mover is self-evident, and the thing moved is the sense organ.

Everything that is changed (moved) is potentially the thing into which it is changed, and so the sense has the potentiality of sense-perception, and, as has been explained in many places, potentiality is in matter[68]. Let us therefore: consider which matter should be this potentiality.

So, we say; Matter is predicated *per prius* of the first and common and transitory matter. This matter is potentially that thing which it ought to receive. Although it is in its essence without form, it is, as we have said, connected with a form,[69] and, therefore, it takes always one of the contraries. This is because the first forms which are the forms of the substances, such as lightness and heavyness[70], are never without contraries. The same applies to the accidents that are related to the bodies *qua* bodies, since matter possesses of the first accidents only one of the contraries,[71] and the first of the accidents to exist in it is extension (= lengths). Hence, matter always exists as corporeal. But, the cause of the extension being the first accident inherent in matter has been given elsewhere. Next, there are other kinds *viz.* quality, place and the rest of the ten categories which apply to the body. Every form that is in matter then has necessarily extension. For form belongs either to a simple body and, as has been said, has extension because of the matter, or belongs to *matters* which have extension. And, in so far as it is a form it will necessarily have the kind of extension which it has, no matter whether the relations of its three dimensions to one another were determined, as in the case of animals, or whether it has them for the form accidentally, like a piece of gold, since a piece of gold may be globular having all three dimensions equal, and when it is extended and becomes oblong, its dimensions are nearer to one another.

The sensibles are accidents in material bodies, and are those that are peculiar to natural bodies or the forms of natural bodies. The natural accidents are either characteristics of natural bodies, like heat, cold, hardness, and softness, or common to both natural and artificial bodies. But they are for the artificial bodies *per posterius* and for the natural bodies *per prius.* The sensibles are then forms in natural bodies, the accidents being taken as forms. It is evident that all these are *immattered* forms, the forms of none of them being separable.

Natural accidents are either movers or moved. Movers, again, are either homogeneous[72] to the thing moved namely, the thing that becomes like them, like fire; or not homogeneous, like fire for hardening clay.

That which is moved from its species however, does not become that mover nor acquires the form that is peculiar to the mover in so far as it is that mover. Hence, the natural attributes are set in motion towards the species.[73] Now if they were moved towards that particular individual of the species of the mover it would. not be possible for it to change (=move) a single piece of wood, but their movement is caused by fire itself, like the movement of the lover for the beloved. For this movement does not set any man in motion at random, for example, a man *qua* man; and this is self-evident.

Hence it is clear about the mover that it moves not because it is that which is in matter in so far as it is in matter, but it moves in so far as it is that species, as is observed in the mixed bodies which are set in motion by the movement of the dominating part without having, at the time of mixing, any choice. Nor is there any discrepancy except if there are two contraries (to be mixed). But here there is only one contrary, and matter has no meaning in it; but it is in the body as though it were a non-existent, and form were alone in the body; its nature has already been explained as we mentioned[74] while discussing change. But this being is not the same through which change has occurred, but is the being of the form that characterises it for the sake of its essence.

Now if this form exists while being separated from the matter in the way we described[75] then the form must be in one of the two ways : either it is so that it had been a different changed existent and then appeared to perception—this is evidently absurd, for it necessarily follows from this that the form of " this particular scribe ", for instance, must be present to the sense organ before the perception of the object of sense[76]—, or it is so that it is in the process of becoming, which necessarily entails of its being potentially before. And what is potential is matter. But if this matter belongs to the one " becoming " then the one becoming is the same as the object, because it necessarily follows that the " becoming " must be a body, and in sense-perception it will have size in itself. Thus, the small will not stimulate that which is greater than it, otherwise the part will not be smaller than the whole which is absurd.

If at all, matter is only connected with the mover by a connection different from the first connection. If matter is in a different state so that when it is in a certain state the mover is connected with it, and when in a certain other state it is not connected with it—this state being the soul—or, there are matters of not a single species, then, how can a matter be without a form at all ? How can that whose nature is this be moved, and how did it come to be ? For this mover is connected with this object of movement in a way different from the way it is connected with matter so that the forms would start to receive, since we cannot hold that sensation moves the sensible.[77] If we held what Galen held concerning sights then the sensible would act and would surely be separable. But Galen maintains that the moved mover moves towards the mover, namely, the sensible,[78] while Aristotle ascertains that the mover here is the sensible which is moved in a way towards the thing moved, because the mover must be actual. This is self-evident. And this potentiality, in general, is the soul.

Since the facts are, as has been shown, (we say :) everything that is becoming and perishable is a tangible body. All tangible body is either simple or compound. The simple bodies are the four which have been enumerated in many places—one of these places being in the twelfth book of the *book of Animals*.[79] As has been shown, every sentient body is compound[80] and not simple, and as described, it is made of earth in order to have a stature and a specific limit, because there is no animal having parts similar to each other and to the whole, nor any plant. Everything that is composite has its elements of which it is composed either actually in it—its composition being then either by contiguity or by coalescence, and in general, joined together— or in potentiality, its composition being then mixture. Everything that possesses soul is composed in this way and not in any of the other ways. For there is no plant nor any animal in which any of the elements exists actually, and so there is not one element manifest in it in a way as to believe that " this " is one of the two, as is ascertained in the case of many compound things[81], like many stones and many mineral bodies. On the contrary, earth and water are the only elements that are found in plants and animals mixed together. But the rest of the elements is sometimes hidden one in the other.

All that is mixed has an agent to mix it,[82] and how simply mixing takes place has been shown in the *De Generatione et Corruptione.*[83]

Mixing is either artificial, like the mixing of gold and silver; and of honey and of vinegar in oxymel; or natural as the mixing of the elements in plants. As shown, natural mixing is caused by action and by " being acted upon ".

The kinds of change by which each single kind of mixing takes place are either boiling, putrefaction or some other kinds of those enumerated in *Meteorology IV*.[84] All these kinds are completed by natural heat[85] which is necessarily in a natural body because heat is a separable thing. This heat is not in one of the elements since if it were in it, it would necessarily require to be moved in space together with an other element so that they would eventually meet each other, because meeting precedes mixing. Now, if the mover of both or of one of them does not move in order to mix them then it is an accidental mixing.

Sometimes mixing takes place and sometimes not,[86] because the cold element is sometimes in efficient in capacity so that it cannot move the other element which is hot; then the hot element moves it or makes it like itself.

This is, however, genesis and not mixing.[87] And, sometimes, it takes place according to each of them moving the other, but this does not happen always in one and the same relation, and so it produces various kinds of mixing. Hence, when the matter happens according to order it needs necessarily a mover from without. The expression محرک is derived from تحریک (to move) which is تدبیر (to manage), so necessarily it needs a manager.

The artificial mixing is included in this kind, and it is through this kind of mixing only that the mixed object always becomes potentially a medium between the things which constitute the mixture. For the one that mixes and moves the object of mixing in this way makes the mixed thing stop in one of the intermediaries; and the thing mixed becomes intermediary things only because it is homogeneous to the elements.

But when the agent that causes mixing is "warmth" which is homogeneous to the "heat" of the elements then it causes something like boiling (= concoction) that produces mineral bodies[88] provided it so happens that the matter is suitable for being boiled. This kind of mixing resembles the artificial mixing that employs fire, as *e.g.* the part mixed of earth and water. In this mixing things become manifest which are not to be found in the elements, as condensation and rarefaction,[89] as it happens in the case of gold; and similar to this accident are odours and flavours, and the different colours, and in short, the bodily states that spread over the body and are divided by its division. It follows necessarily then that they must have parts similar to each other and to the whole, because boiling sometimes occurs in them. This is a kind of mixing which is not like the first. Hence, spherical movements does not produce a mineral body and, in general, a body having its parts alike, except in special places, because mineral bodies are not produced but from a mine. A mine is a place in the cavity of the earth where a body having parts similar to one another is generated through vapour and smoke that are confined to it in order to thicken that part of the earth which boils by the heat that is in the part itself.[90] It is therefore that there is not at all in all the three places enumerated in the *Meteorology* any organic body.

Then, the things produced by mixing that exist with this kind of fetidness can only exist having different elements.[91] All this is either a natural form, or accidents in natural bodies to be found in the definition of the near mover.

But in that which is composed of the elements, which is moved by the heavenly bodies, and in general, that which is moved by locomotion which causes meeting, the near and the far mover are one and the same, namely, the spherical body, since it moves by nature and essentially. But the near mover in what is produced by broiling is the heat by which broiling takes place, and the far mover is the body that is moved in a circle Hence , in what is produced by broiling the near mover from the elements is either one of the elements, namely, fire, or that which is composed of fire. All these are sensible things, either primary like colours, or secondary, like extension (=lengths), shapes and forms of natural substances. All these are things which exist in matter, and when they are in matter they become with the matter one in number and different in potentiality, as we have described before.[92]

None of these things can have sense-perception. The primary matter is each and every one of these potentialiy. Everything that becomes one with matter belongs to the matter either primarily, or secondarily, or thirdly. Those forms that belong to matter essentially are necessarily substances, because the rest of the matter that exists depends only on the forms of substances, and hence, they need alteration when they are generated. For matter is not at all anything in actuality,[93] but the thing that suffers change necessarily exists as a definite thing in actuality ; and hence, when set in motion it necessarily exists, requires a form[94] and undergoes a change in the accident, and it exists through the form that is in it. This causes change in form just as the movement of place causes change of positions. For movement was not in the position, but position is caused through movement. If, however, movement were in the form then matter itself would be moved,[95] and, thus, would become a certain thing. But in the case of alteration the matter is moved by accident.

As we have said, all that exists in the natural bodies whether element or mineral, is material and united with matter. But plants and animals have those material states which belong to the elements,[96] . like the material states that are caused by broiling. These states bring into being those bodies that have parts similar to one another and are constituted of the elements Besides, animals and plants have some other states which do not belong to the elements nor are caused by broiling of the elements. This is the forming of a new thing which is evident in most of plants, and is clearer in animals, and they have parts similar to each other because they are organs.

The mover that causes this motion of matter, namely, the creation of a new thing is a different kind of mover. This is evident by a slight consideration. As shown in *Physics VIII*,[97] this mover is not the sphérical movement although it is not without it. But the mover seeks only the particular essential movement which is the near one.

This mover is, therefore, not the broiling heat, but the broiling heat is its organ, and hence, flavour, smell and the rest of the accidents caused by broiling are inherent in bodies. But how these accidents are caused by the broiling heat has been explained in *Meteorology IV*.[98] These accidents therefore necessarily give rise to the forming of a new thing.

In that which has such a principle, at the time when it is generated, the mover must necessarily be *mind* But this view is more suitable to the genesis of animate beings, as has been summarized in the seventeenth book of the *book of Animals*.[99]

That which has this principle is of two kinds : one kind connected with its organ by which it causes motion, as for instance, the animal that propagates itself. This is the semen, because the semen is a body that generates the animate. And it is evident that the heat of the semen through which the semen acts is in it.

As to the other kind, its organ by which it is moved is in something else. This applies to those animals which are said to be generated spontaneously. The organ that belongs to a kind like this is the heat of putrefaction or some other heat. This kind somehow resembles the productive art, because the organs of art are outside the body to which the art is applied. Hence, it causes motion through moving the elements and mixing.

This heat continues to move the earth which is mixed with water until when the whole has reached a state in which it can receive that form, it receives it eventually. It is evident that with the beginning of motion it starts to receive the form. Receiving and moving corresponding mutually with each other. The soul when perfected receives the form of the mixture and receives it through the " mixing " it possesses.

The form which the mixed bodies receive either does not move anything essentially, but is received, and this is like the forms of the minerals. And again, this form precedes in matter that which exists in the matter through the form like the states that characterize the gold in so far as it is gold, *e.g* rarefaction and endurance to the fire. Or it moves the body that contains it with a movement peculiar to the body, as for instance, the soul of the plant. For when matter receives the form of a definite body it moves that body together with itself. Here are then necessarily immattered faculties some of which are far, as for example, the power of the elements, and some near, as for example, the power of the mixed body which is always found only connected with form, and so it is always a substratum. Hence, for the animate there is no opposite, because this form has no particular privation. There is a privation only of that form, as for instance, you say: "The form of the bee". Now, some of the forms have "far matter", as is said of the water "extremely hot".

As to the near faculty, it is never without form, because it is always a substratum and is not at all separable. Hence, it is likely that the form of the mineral is in its matter, because it has no contraries nor opposing privations *e.g.* the opposition of privation to habit.

In such cases the form of "mixing" is the quiddity of that body, as for instance, gold. For the mixed object is the matter and its existence is the species of condensation. It is evident that this condensation is in the near matter which is in the mixed object like the form for the natural composition (mixing). This matter then receives that condensation, but since the matter is not at all separable from this form, the "aggregate" of all these is always like a single thing, matter being manifest in existence only at the time of change. All these are forms in the matter through which the "aggregate" becomes a single thing, since this is the meaning of matter's receiving forms that arise in the matter.[100] But when the form becomes different, and this is only when it is separated in a way, then it is different from matter.

If the difference is caused by what takes place then it necessarily follows that it is through a preceding change either in the form or in another substratum,[101] as has been shown in *Physics VIII*.[102]

But form cannot suffer change, since all that is changed is divisible[103] and form has no parts[104] nor is body. And hence, change occurs in a different thing. Thus form, through changing from this form, acquires a limited relation. So, form is changed by accident[105]—its change being in a moment just as it happens to that which is related. For, although being greater, if AB is not twice of JD then JD is necessarily only a half, and AB twice without having been changed in itself ; it remains rather in its state as it has been, but is changed from one relation to another relation.

All change, as explained in *Physics VIII*,[106] is in quantity, in quality, in place, or depends on one of these. But when form is separated from matter, that same form exists actually, while being what it is, separated in an existence peculiar to it,[107] and is different from that which it was while being in the matter which received it. Now, had it existed[108] without having come to be then this would entail necessarily an absurdity, namely, that the form of a specified individual should exist before it exists either in sense-perception and imagination—which is impossible—or in mind—which is assumed to be possible ; but we shall explain this when we shall investigate about the rational faculty.

Now, it is clear that sensation has an origin. All that has origin potentially before it comes to be But how is it possible for sensation to be a separable form as well as to "become", since "becoming" concerns matter only?

We answer: Our expression "matter" applied to the faculties of the soul as well as to the faculties of the body is equivocal, because matter exists in the bodies only by being specified by this form, so that they both become a single thing that demands the performance of the action that is that this existing thing should perform, by its nature as has been explained before this. By the expression "matter" in this place, we mean only the reception of the form through which the body which has a potency like this becomes sentient, since both the material faculty and the faculty which is soul accept colour, and colour is form in the matter—colour and matter being one thing—as " this colour " on its own has no existence at all. Colour in the faculty of sensation is that which exists with what characterizes it. It has left its matter and become a definite thing. Hence, it is not possible for matter to receive two contraries like whiteness and blackness, the two contraries, because if it were to receive the two contraries, then the two contraries would surely be in matter, and there would be no contrariety between them at all, but they are essentially contraries, for they are essentially two forms, each of them or both forms different from each other. Hence, it is not possible for them to exist except in two ways. That they are in two substrata is possible; but if they are in one substratum, then they must be in it in two different moments without meeting in one substratum. Since they are in the sensitive faculty as two separate beings their co-existence is not impossible; what is impossible is only their being together in one substratum, and not that they cannot co-exist in a genus, and in general, in the faculties of the soul. But this exists materially only in colours. For one and the same air, for example, is between white and black at the same time. This is because their forms are not in the same way in air as form is in matter, but are in a way intermediate between the material reception and the reception of the psychical faculty.

Since faculties are defined by relations of the substratum to the habit and the faculties are distinguished through this from each other in their essence, the sensitive faculty is a preparedness in the sense organ which becomes the form of the thing perceived. The difference between المعنى (the meaning) and الصورة (the form)[109] is this that form and matter become one thing without existing separately, whereas the " meaning " of the thing perceived is a form separated from matter.[110] So, the " meaning " is the form separated from matter. Hence, the psychical faculty must receive the "meaning" while it is a " meaning ", and that which receives is a " meaning " in potentiality. Similarly, the perception of the soul is in no way a passive state. But whether it comes to be by " being acted upon ", we shall soon explain later on. It is therefore sometimes assumed that the one that is " being acted upon " receives form alone, and that when the potentially hot, for example, becomes actually hot it does not receive the " meaning " of that which is in the mover, although things are from the mover, as we said before.[111] It receives only an other hot and so it becomes a different " hot " resembling the first, while there is no relation between the heat that is in one of the two and the heat that is in the other in any way. The only relation between them is this, that their respective forms when separated become one in number. As to the difference between their two individual forms, if it is permissible to call the individual of heat a form, there is no difference between these two forms and the matter when it becomes an individual, as has been summarized somewhere else [112] Hence, in saying "the heat of the one of the two" we do not mean that it is with its matter so that the individual of the "heat" itself should be in the soul.

Since the "meaning" of the thing is the thing and since the meaning of "thing" is its actual existence, it means to us when the meaning of an individual reaches us that we have perceived the individual through that faculty that belongs to us.

It is evident that the perceptions of the material beings we acquire are transitory. If they were not transitory then they would be eternal. But if they were eternal it would necessarily imply that Zayd, for example, was before Zayd, and "this hot" was before "this hot"; it will also imply that they are moved in space, and other similar absurdities.

Again, it is generally admitted that sensations are transitory. This can be ascertained if we give some slight attention to it. All that is transitory has existed potentially before its actual existence. As we said before,[113] possibility and potentiality are inter-dependent. This potentiality is then necessarily in a matter, and this matter is the matter of the like of this being. And, customarily it is called spiritual[114] and non-corporeal, or similar terms are used, and hence, it does not become a body when perceived, because body is there only when the form is not at all different—this is so when it is not separated.

Someone may ask about perceptions and say: " Is the form, when it is different, in the matter which contains it? If this is so then the matter would exist actually while not being matter. How can then that which is not a body be connected with that which is a body except by becoming a form in it? But if there is no difference and the case is like its existence in matter then it is not separated".

We reply: That the perceptions are in a substratum is clear, because if they were not in a substratum they would not come to be. But that the perceptions and the substratum are one and the same thing is so, and in this way perception becomes particular. For if they were completely different from the substratum then they would certainly be a species or intelligible. We shall soon explain this when we shall turn to the discussion of the rational faculty, since the discussion here is on the soul and its faculties.

But that it follows from what has been posited that form does not exist free from matter, is no necessary inference from what has been posited, but it is open to doubt that the being of the form suffers a change. This is because the matter, as we said before, exists only in relation to that of which it is matter. The power of perception is to receive the form as separated in its particular existence. Then the matter of perception is by nature the reception of the forms of the apprehensibles The mover of the matter is the object of perception in so far as it is perceived For it is clear from the nature of these material forms that they essentially possess this power, and this movement belongs to them for the sake of their particular being. Hence, this power is in the active form like heat and cold, and in the passive form like hardness and softness. For that which causes the movement related to the passive state also causes movement to it while it is in a substratum, and it moves another matter of the species of the matter that is in it. The relation of this matter to the "meaning" is like the relation of the matter that is in that mover to the form itself that is in the species. The matter of perception is related to the form in a different way that characterises it, and hence, it is matter in the equivocal sense of the term. But the matter of the perceptibles is called matter *per prius*, and this (*i e.* the matter of perception) is called matter only *per posteritus* and in relation to the moving sensible, *e.g.* the hot and the cold.

The mover then has at first two kinds of movement for two kinds of matter—one, for the matter of the species of its matter, and the other for the matter through which it (*i e.* the mover) is sensed. This movement belongs to that which has a body not in so far as it is that body. Hence, the perception of the small and large body is the same,[115] especially, their imagination. We shall soon explain why it is so later on.

Perception varies in excellence only in so far as it is strong or weak.

We have said what the perceptive faculty, in general, is. This faculty is a soul which exists in the animate body and is the form of the temperament of the animated body. The mixed body which possesses this faculty is animate and alive.

Since all generation is either change or dependent on change, as shown in the *Physics*,[116] it is necessary that perception must be so. Since all that is changed is divisible[117] and perception is not divisible, it necessarily follows that this faculty is connected with a body either by itself or through a connecting medium.

Psychical perceptions are of two kinds—sensation and imagination. It is not possible to imagine that which is not sensed, and hence, for example, it is not possible to imagine " colour ". Sense-perception therefore precedes imagination by nature, for it is like matter for the imagination. So sense-perception is the first perception connected with the body. It is then necessary that there is no sense-perception without imagination but the change is not in the sensible. Change is the form of the sensing. The sensing is then necessarily a body whose form is the sensitive faculty. Sense-perception, in general, is the potency of a body that is acted upon by the sensible and with whose perfection is connected the perfection of the psychical faculty that is in it. Hence, it is necessarily implied that the sensible is that which causes imagination and the sensitive is the object of imagination. Hence, " heat " and "cold" are sensed themselves and primarily. As for " hardness ", softness and smoothness, we shall soon explain their nature in the discourse on the faculty of touch, since this is the discourse on sense-perception, in general.

Since not every power moves every body, and movements are many, senses are many to respond to their respective movements. Since the movement through which sensation is caused is for the sake of the form only, and the form exists through many things, it follows necessarily that in sense-perception those forms must be imprinted without being separated from one another.

Since that by which the thing is constituted is either common or particular[118]—the particular being only perceived by one sense, and the common by those senses on which the common object depends, it is not sensed primarily as, for instance, extension (= lengths) and shapes.

Since the form is joined accidentally by many other things, these things are therefore not impressed in the sense organ ; they are sensed accidentally, like colour, because colour is connected with the fact that it is, for example, in the scribe ; and so it is said that the scribe is seen accidentally. The sensing animal very often commits error about these accidents. But how this faculty exists in animals has been described in the discussion on the generation of animals, and that is in the sixteenth book of the *book of Animals*.[119]

This is sense-perception, in general.

As described, the sensibles are, in general, either common or particular. The particular, as shown before, is that by which the sense organ is acted upon, and the common is that by which the sense organ is not acted upon, but exists potentially only when the form is perceived. Hence, it is said that the common sensibles are perceived only by the common sense, because the sense is not affected by them. They belong only to this faculty (not) because they are connected with the sense organ, but in so far as they are actual, for the faculty, when separated from the sense organ, becomes the common sense. It is separated from the sense organ only when it becomes a certain thing, and that is by perceiving a sensed object ; the sense is then necessarily in sense-perception, as has been shown before.[120] Hence, this faculty cannot be without the sensibles entirely, because it is in a body. But that which is absurd is to make it separable without any connection with a body. This is one of the absurdities that necessarily follows from the doubt recorded before this.

Let us, now, speak of the kinds of sense-perception.

CHAPTER IV

DISCOURSE ON SIGHT

As shown before,[1] the soul is the first entelechy whose matter is the natural mixture of the body. I mean by my expression "first" [2] the same as one speaks of a geometer when he is not practising geometry, or a musician when he is not displaying the art of music, and by "last" something like that which is said of a musician when he produces a tune. For the first entelechy is always like matter for the last entelechy, and so it needs necessarily something else to bring it into actuality, namely, a mover, since everything moved has a mover. But the mover in the soul is hidden while the mover in sense-perception is manifest, just as it happens to a polished mirror. For having been polished is the first entelechy, and so, whenever and object of sight is present, its shape is reflected in the mirror which is not changed into anything else in order to become nearer (to the object), such as it takes place in the iron in so far as it is iron,[3] since it requires polishing, and hence, one does not say of the iron that it is a first entelechy. In short, the first entelechy is the preparedness of the body to receive something without being changed essentially, not accidentally, because the mirror is sometimes changed, *e.g.* it is turned to face the object of sight.

The faculty of sight is then the first entelechy of the eye, namely, the visual soul. But when it does see, it becomes vision which is its name in its last entelechy. The same applies to the remaining faculties. For, when a faculty is isolated and is mere potency, it is a soul, and hence, an embryo as well as a sleeping person is said to have soul,[4] but when it performs its actions, it is an actual sense-perception. Hence, the faculty through which, for example, vision takes place is potentially the objects seen.

As said before,[5] the sensibles are prior and are peculiar to each sense—some of them being common and others accidental.

The first sensible for sight is colour, and therefore, it is perceived only by the eye. Hence, the organ of the body that perceives colour contains vision, wherever and in which form whatsoever it may be, because a body is defined only by its function, and hence, a statue is not a man, nor is a sharp sound a knife, since they do not perform the actions of the species in whose name they share [6] Hence, it is said that "eye" is predicated of the eye of the alive and the eye of the dead equivocally, and not univocally.

The visual soul is then the faculty that exists in the eye and through which the eye perceives colour. This faculty is located in the vitreous humour.[7] This is evident from the symptoms to be observed in "formation of cataract" in the eye. Hence, it is necessary to investigate the nature of colour.

We say: Colour can only be perceived through the mediation of air. Hence, if it is placed upon the eye, the eye cannot perceive it.[8] And air cannot serve the eye in perceiving colour except if it is together with light,[9] either because colours in darkness are potential and have no existence, or because the air receives colours only through the vision in which the colours are.

That colour is in darkness is evident, when colours are observed in the shade, in the sun and in the condition that occurs to plants when clouds pass over them, coming between them and the sun, since their colours vary a great deal, as has been summarized in the *De Sensu et Sensatu.*[10] So it is necessary that we should proceed and explain what colour is.

The illuminant is that which gives light and the illuminated is that which has light—light being the entelechy of the illuminated in so far as it is illuminated.

The illuminant is said in two ways,[11] *per prius et posterius.* The first is that in which we assume that the sun shares together with fire. That which is said *per posterius* is that which imparts light through being illuminated from elsewhere. This is through reflection of light, as it arises in the case of the moon and of transparent bodies, and this is of various kinds. That which cannot make others visible[12] is the kinds of the terrestrial things, *e g.* what one sees in the water when oars fall in it at night, the scale of some fish, and the fire of the fire-flies, but these are not colours[13] and are effects in the eye, as has been explained elsewhere.

Light then is that which is in the air in the presence of a body that has this state is the illuminated.

But the question whether the sun itself exists or its effect in the world that comprises animate beings is an object of investigation, and is very difficult indeed. For a man who is in water sees the sun on the surface of the water and finds it so near that he assumes that it is actually on the surface of the water. Similarly, it may happen to a man on the sea-shore at the time of sun-rise or sun-set when by chance a dense smoke from a place close to the observer arises that he assumes that the sun is in the smoke, and hence, he sees it as large sized and red and yellow. Again, when we look into fire and its states through which it becomes illuminant, we find that it is through the mean between density and rarity. This is clear by what we said [14] about shooting-stars and the comets. But the fact is, as Aristotle says in the seventeenth book of the *book of Animals*[15] that the form of fire is visible—this is when he promises us to discuss about fire—so let us leave it for the place that suits the discussion of such things.

That which is received is always in contact with the qualities that are in the recipient, and hence, the saying goes :—

> "As through he were looking into the sword through its length ";[16]

and the same happens to extension (lengths), as has been demonstrated in the book of *Mathematical Sights and Shades* wherein the causes have been given.

It is clear and evident that the fire received by air is simple fire. It is received either immediately or through the medium of something contained in it. If at all, this something is only analogically said of having " being ".

Of the contraries that do not exist together in the same substratum, as heat and cold, for example, some are absolutely not found in the same substratum, as even and odd numbers, since " five ", for example, will under no circumstances become an even number. Others are such that they are not in the same substratum at the same time, as *e.g.* hot and cold, blindness and sight. Others are such that are in the same substratum at the same time—this is the case with many species of Relation, as the kinds of related position, such as right and left; and hence, " becoming " in their substrata is not a change, but follows a change[18]. Change is only in the " now ".[9] and not at all in any length of time, and how this is meant, has been shown in the *Physics*.

Position and Relation are either essential, that is by nature, (or by accident). That which is by nature is like the position of some limbs of the animal in relation to others, and so you do find that nature has achieved in each of them or in one of them something through which the position finds its perfection. That which is accidental is not like this, as *e.g.* the position of Zaid to ' Amr. As explained in the *Physics*, position is not a faculty that spreads over the body,[20] since the position of A to G B is like its position to H D, and whichever part is taken from G B, A's position to it will necessarily be the same.

The illuminant with reference to the illuminated is a form and possesses relation. Bodies possess position absolutely only through their surface that surrounds them from the outside. Hence, the bodies have position through their surface.

Sometimes, the things related have no such two substrata which contain two individuals of the same species of relation, as *e.g.* begetting, because the begotten is not the begetter of the one who begot him. But sometimes, there are in between the two substrata two individuals of the same species, as in the case of coming to blows and cultivating friendship with one another. That which has no two individuals in between its two substrata has sometimes a kind of relation in between them which distinguishes one from the other, *e.g.* if one animal is on the right side of an other animal. For when H, for example, is on the right side of B, B must be on the left side of H, since both of them have right and left. But that which is not an animal is not like this, since to be on the right side of a mountain, for example, is not to be on the left side from it, because a mountain has no right nor left except in an analogous sense.

The illuminant has a position relative to the illuminated, and so whenever it is present it must necessarily have it, and to receive by nature this position to it is a relation. That which gives light is that which has a nature like this.

Relation in so far as it is relation is not divisible by the parts of the body. For relation is a nature common to that which is body and that which is not body. Hence, it is sometimes not divisible by the parts of the body in its essence.

Since illumination produces a relation between two bodies, every part of the illuminant has with every part of the illuminated this relation—no matter whether it is possible for them or not possible. Hence, all that is illuminated does not necessarily give light; but how much light it ever gives, is then a definite degree of relation ; but sometimes it does not illuminate the whole of it but it necessarily illuminates the part which is near to it Its nature has already been explained in the discussion on the reflection of rays.[21] So, we have said what is light, and what is illuminated, and what is illuminant.

It is thereby clear how light exists in the air without time, and how the air is illuminated by the sun and a lamp in the same period of time—if this is to be called time—and in view of the differerence of dimensions as they are. It is also clear how the same air is illuminated by two sources of light that are in opposite position, while the effect of the one is not distinct from that of the other, such as if either of the two sources of light be on different ends of the sides of a square, and between them an obstacle that intersects them so that the centre alone is illuminated by the two sources of light together. Now if the light ray is not reflected, then the diagonal of the state of one luminary which falls on the diagonal of the other will not be straight. Similarly, to one who is in the middle of the side of the square the state of either of the two luminaries will not be clear.

Since colour, as shown in the *De Sensu et Sensatu*,[22] comes about through the mixture of the illuminated with the body which has colour in the manner I have explained there, colour is also a luminary in a way, and moves the air. Colour moves what is illuminated but in so far as it is illuminated, since the illuminated is the mover of this colour.

But how is it said that colour moves the translucent in actuality? This is in so far as the colour is received only in so far as it is illuminated and to receive the illuminant is related to illumination. Hence, its setting colour in motion is illumination and translucence. Here becomes clear the error of one[23] who believes that to see in vacuum is more possible than that what appears to sense-perception in water and in air. But the matter is quite the reverse of what Democritus has assumed, since if air were eliminated there could be no seeing at all

Just as colour is not perceived without light[24] so light cannot be perceived except in connection with colour. This is evident by what we said before.[25]

Now, colour is simple, and the simple possesses a shape necessarily. Hence, vision perceives shape and length, and in short, all that is found in the constitution of colour or in the constitution of that by which colour is constituted. Hence, vision perceives the substances that are the substrata of the colours.

Since causes are either near, namely, those that characterize the essential, or far and are enumerated among the accidents; the same applies to the objects of sight, for example, lengths and the like which are essential for the eye, and substances that are accidental.

But that which is particularly accidental is that which is perceived through the mediation of another faculty. The white, for example, is an effect to us and so it does not belong to the eye neither as near nor as far.

Sometimes it is assumed that what is essential is often found in mirrors, since shape and movement are manifest in them, and also other states of the coloured, but they are not in them in the same way, as has been summarized elsewhere.

The movement that. is manifest in mirrors is not a movement that has arisen but is reflections in the mirrors, because the part that is manifest in the state A is not the same that is manifest to B so that it would be a movement. This is only like the shadow of the thing moved, for shadow is privation of light, not of movement, because a shadow has no movement.

As already said,[27] sense-perception is a matter that receives the form of the object of sense-perception, hence, it receives the impression of that by which the form is constituted, whatever be its nature.

But the mirror does not receive the form, but it receives the images of some of the properties that have form.

CHAPTER V

DISCOURSE ON HEARING

The faculty of hearing is the entelechy of the sense of hearing, and its function[1] is to apprehend the impression arising in the air by the impact of the two bodies mutually impinging upon each other. This is the state in which a certain thing is heard and its sensation is called "hearing". This is because all the bodies that produce sound are either hard or moist. If they are hard, then whenever struck by a body, they produce sound. But if the body is moist[2] then it does not produce sound except when the movement of the striking body towards the object struck is faster[3] than the dissipation of the moist so that the movement impinges upon the body. Now the body that contains this movement is set in motion and recoils from the motion, and the motion rebounds from the body in all directions adjacent to the place where the striking body and the struck have come in contact. Although rebounding from the striking body, the air receives from the striking body an impression peculiar to it, as is evident in the vibrating bodies.

The effect of this sensation in the strings of the lute is obvious, because we find that when we move *bamm* (the bass or the fourth string, having the deepest tone) in the level of *mutlaq* (the open-string) that which is *mathna* (the dual chord) is moved, but that which is on *zīr* (the first string) is not moved, nor is that which is on *mathlath* (the triplet chord). Similarly, when *mathlath* (the triplet chord) is struck *zīr* (the first string) is not affected. If we put our fingers on the *sabbāba* (the first-finger) of *zīr*, then this will move only that which is on it; and the same happens to the scale which is equal in pitch (المتسا وية الطبقة), since it is alike in parts. Exactly the same happens to "that which is general" and "what is general" is similar in parts, and not equal.

The first sensible is the impression[4] that is in air or in water caused by an impact ; but it is connected with a movement and is not possibly perceived without the air being moved. Hence, it is an impression connected with the motion caused by the air in the impression,[5] and hence, it follows that what reverberates from a body is the same but not in the same state. It is, therefore, necessary for the two contraries to undergo a certain change, but the impression remains one and the same.

Similarly in the human ear particularly, since the mutual impinging is frequent in it, the air suffers various kinds of reverberation[6] and the sound remains, as it happens in the instruments that produce sound, as for example, the lute. It is through this that a sound becomes a musical note, for the musical note is a sound that remains apprehensible for a time ; and hence, not every sound is a musical note. It is for this reason that when a sound is followed by another sound the two particles of air are mixed together while they are in different states, and produce a mixed note, either agreeable or disagreeable. This is the reason through which the rhythmic modes render the agreeable disagreeable and the disagreeable agreeable. This is the case in the lute the "moaning" of which is a note. All this has been explained elsewhere.

Since the first place of hearing is air, because it is the first recipient of sound, hence the two bodies mutually impinging upon each other are sensible by accident, and hence, error occurs in hearing them, as occurs to sight concerning what belongs to its substratum by accident, as has been explained before.[7] Hence, sometimes many sounds arise in different bodies and are believed to be one sound, as for example, the sound made by water falling on a hollow and smooth body sounds to the ear exactly like the sound produced by the lute so that he who listens to it, but does not see it, assumes that some strings of a lute are being played on. This is how the jugglers are able to make us believe of thunder, and the mimics to produce sounds of various bodies so that we assume that these bodies exist while they do not exist.

And it is the characteristic of that which concerns a particular sense accidentally that the other senses come to its help, and this particular sensible is apprehended in this way. We shall soon explain after this how that is and due to which faculty.

Some bodies are sounding and some not sounding. Those that are sounding are the bodies that possess an organ to produce sound, their mover being the "modification" that arises in them. These are those bodies that possess soul[8] and have lungs, namely the animate which breathes.

The animal known as the cricket, however, does not produce sound[9] in this way, but it produces sound accidentally. For the air comes out through the oesophagus, and so it produces sound.

But that which does not breathe does not produce sound even when struck by a body. This is how sound takes place.

Since, as we said, sense-perception concerns the form of the sensible, hearing follows upon the form that is in the air and through which it exists, and hence, it follows the way in which sound exists and the rest of its corollaries. It concerns neither shape nor anything else that concerns sight, since this is not in the constitution of sound.

CHAPTER VI

DISCOURSE ON SMELL

As said before, smell is the apprehension of the form of the object of smell. It is located in the nose. It is necessary to proceed according to that way and to investigate what the first recipient of the thing smelt is, and so it will be clear to us what smell essentially is and what belongs to it accidentally in the same way as this has been explained for sight. For colour is the object of sight and the first recipient is simple. As shown, it seems that the remaining three senses are of a different kind ; and that these senses are far more necessary for the security of the nutrient than the first two. Rightly this is so, because these are states of the mixed body. For colour and the impact of sound necessarily cause change in the mixed body, since they do not belong to it neither accidentally nor essentially. As explained in other places, colour does not depend upon the natural mixture. This has been explained by Alexander of Aphrodisias.[1]

The first object of smell is odour Let us therefore say what odour is. That everything odorous is mixed is clear when we investigate bodies. Mixing[2] therefore precedes smell in the body by nature. But that, although prior by nature, mixing is essential is also clear by examining odour and its generation, as happens with colours, since investigation is made concerning only the parts and certainty is attained concerning the whole. And the fact about such things, as Abū Naṣr says, is that they become certain at time, while they are different at other times in " abundance and scarcity ". We observe, for example, in summer in some countries that soil does not smell but when drops of rain fall upon it, it does smell when the rain mixes with it, and particularly when it rains from a near cloud, because the rain is then warm and sometimes snow.

Similarly, again, the existence of taste is prior to odour by nature in an object of smell, and so odour seems to be almost identical with taste ; and hence, the taste of many things is apprehended from their odour. Most irrational animals use only this sense to gain their livelihood,[3] as it is to be found in vultures, in dogs and other animals. The horse, for example, recoils from his food when it smells differently from its natural odour. And hence, this sense is strong in animals and weak[4] in man, because the animal needs it most.

It is the characteristic of this sense that many animals cannot make their sense of smell work unless they inhale air[5], namely, those which have lungs[6]. For if a smelling object is placed on the nose they do not perceive it[7] unless they inhale. Sometimes odour moves the air at such a distance from the person who inhales that it is not moved by the air of respiration, and this is clearly observed.

This sense organ has a curtain[8] on it which is not lifted. But when inhaling takes place the curtain is lifted and the object of smell reaches the sense organ. Hence, when he who smells intends to take the smell in he does not breathe all at once, but breathes in a long time or inhales intermittently.

It is evident that the recipient of odour is, in short, not only homogeneous to air, but also to smoke or vapour that belongs incidentally to perfumes and many cooked things. All these have been specified in the *De Sensu et Sensatu*[9]. And this is why odours of objects remain in many smooth bodies even after their disappearance, for example, the fragrance of wine and honey remains for a long time in brass-vessels after they have been cleaned. Thus in containers the odours of the objects kept in them last long, and hence, sometimes the things that have the same odours are identified by the sense of smell, as happens with hearing.[10] For the things that are perceived by these two senses and their first recipients are separable from the object that causes them. This is not the case with sight nor with touch, and hence, both of them perceive dimensions and shapes more than this (i.e. the sense of smell).

As for taste, we shall soon explain what it is. As shown in other places and as we said before, the mixed body arises from broiling or without broiling, as it happens with gold and silver, and that which is broiled. Broiling is said in general and in particular. When it is said in general it is like a genus for the thing and for cooking; and when it is said in particular it is synonymous with cooking.

It has been shown that broiling takes place only in things mixed of moisture and dryness. When the heat has broiled it somehow there arises in the body something which is called taste. Hence all that tastes has some moisture. Now if by chance it has another mixture of moisture and dryness which are mixed with it and are broiled in a way, then that which arises as a result of this is odour, as has been explained in the *De Sensu et Sensato*.[11]

It is clear that odour arises when the moisture washes[12] the dry that has a quality and is broiled by the heat in a way, and hence it is found in plants more than in animals and stones.

The result of the mixture of that moisture with the dryness which the heat has broiled—for instance, a tree—has a manifest odour of its own. What has no manifest odour, but is odorous potentially needs for this reason fire and heat. Hence, when this kind of odorous object is rubbed or peeled off[13] and, in short, when it is heated its scent becomes manifest.[14] For fragrance needs at first a broiling heat which sometimes suffices to produce it, such as musk and liquid storax,[15] and sometimes does not suffice and needs another heat, as, for example, aromatic wood[16] and the gum of the red juniper (red arsenic) and the like.

Since smell is the apprehension of the form of the object of smell, and is identified with the object of smell, smell does not apprehend any other attribute of the properties of the object of smell except taste. Hence, smell is not apprehended except by accident. This is because when it so happens that the object of smell is attended in a way the aspect of smell is accidentally distinguished by it. Hence the aspect of smell is distinguished by the sense of smell by second intention.

CHAPTER VII

DISCOURSE ON TASTE

It has been shown what taste is,[1] and that taste is not possible neither exclusively in moist nor in dry, and hence, we can taste neither ashes nor pure water nor air. But we can taste the water of rivers and the water of the woods because of the dry that is mixed with these waters.

The matter of taste is then moisture,[2] and hence, when the organ of taste is dry you cannot come to taste things which are mainly dry but you can, for the same reason, taste moist things. For taste sets in motion the moisture of the mouth and receives it in the same way as the air receives colour. Moisture moves the sense of taste,[3] and so whenever there is a moist object, the moisture which is contained in it takes the place of the natural moisture. Moisture is thus needed by taste in the first place in order to exist at all, and in the second place in order to be perceived.

This is why the parts of the throat near the uvula[4] have been made to produce the natural moisture through which taste takes place. This (*i.e.* the natural moisture) is mixed of dry and moist parts in a way, and hence, it is viscous. This moisture has no flavour so that its taste does not make it impossible to receive flavours which are contrary to it. Hence, he who suffers from fever finds everything tasting bitter[5]; for the moisture in his mouth is bitter because smoke is mixed with it, as has been explained elsewhere.

Taste is necessary in animals,[6] and so there is no animal that does not have taste except a few, *e.g* the kind of animals that have shells and the sponge of the sea. It is likely that touch alone will be adequate to meet their needs of food, because they are far from being normal animals and are rather like plants.

Hence, the sense of taste does not apprehend any essential property of anything which has flavour except its flavour ; and hence, anything that has flavour becomes more palatable or disagreeable by being more moist or dry, hot or cold. This is self-evident.

CHAPTER VIII

DISCOURSE ON TOUCH

Touch is the faculty of apprehending the tangible. It is sometimes assumed that the tangible is of various kinds,[1] and hence, the faculty of touch is of many kinds, but is in one and the same substratum.

This sense is spread over[2] the human body and has no particular organ, as is the case with the rest of the senses. But it has a recipient of a definite kind, in all animals, namely, the flesh or what replaces it in those which have no flesh.[3] The primary sense[4] of touch is not in the skin. When the skin is removed, the flesh perceives touch not less than the skin perceives it, on the contrary, one should rather assume that it is more susceptible to touch.

As said before, no animal exists without this sense, and through it an animal is an animal. Hence, when this sense is lost, the individual in question is no longer an animal. There is no sense which is found apart from touch.

As shown in the second book of the *De Generatione et Corruptione*,[5] all the objects of touch go ultimately back to hot and cold, moist and dry, and these contraries are such that neither of the two of them can be replaced by the other, since every sense-perception is connected with a pair of contraries.[6] Sometimes, it so happens that the two contraries become substrata for another contrary. Take, for example, colour : its extremes are white and black, and white is the substratum of glittering and brightening[7], and light : its two extremes are transmission and intensity and this is the substratum of the smooth and hard, hidden and apparent.

And just as this sense is one and is accompanied by many faculties so seems to be the case of touch[8]. In short, the faculties follow the existents according to the order of their being. But moist, dry, hot and cold do not mutually interdepend in this manner, since none of them is a substratum of the other, but there is an essentially different succession and interdependence in them, as has been explained in a different discourse.

Since these contrary qualities do not exist separately in the substratum, the faculties of touch are not separable either and are in a single sense organ.

Since every body which comes to be is perishable, it is an object of touch. No substratum can dispense with these contraries, as it is possible with regard to the rest of the contraries, for sometimes there exists a body that has no colour[9], and a body that has no sound, the same applies to smell and taste—therefore the organs of these senses have been made of the like of these bodies. But this was not possible for this sense organ, and so it is "medium" because the "medium" is in no way potentially one of the extremes. Hence, the organ of touch is "medium" between hot and cold, humid and dry. This is why when Galen assumed that the hand is the organ of touch he held that the skin of the hand is "medium" between the extremes, and thus he transferred what belongs to the body that contains the faculty of touch to some organs of touch. This body is the innate heat. Since the body is not a "medium", it was joined with bodies that are called by Aristotle "flux" and by Galen "nerve", because they bring the psychical coldness from the brain. Hence, a limb that is not connected with the flux from the brain is devoid of touch, and hence, liver, kidneys, and arteries which are full of innate pneuma, have no sense of touch.

But how does the psychical coldness arise? For sometimes its reverse is shown. For the organ of the soul is the innate heat. Now coldness is said of extremes and of the intermediates, but that which is in the brain cannot be an extreme, it is only an intermediate which is in between the "medium" and the extreme. The intermediate is only so because it is mixed with the contrary, so this coldness is mixed with the psychical heat. Hence the heat goes to the brain from the heart through the arteries, and the membrane is on the brain which is assuaged by the heat that is moderate due to the coldness of the membrane, and through which it is in that stage. It is therefore psychical in so far as it is heat, not in so far as it is in the stage that is called "extreme".

Sometimes a doubt is expressed about the sense of touch. That is every sense organ is moved by the sensible, as has been summarized in the general discourse on sense-perception.[10] The mover is either near or distant, essential or accidental. The distant is that which is sensible, and the near is that which serves, *e.g.* air for sight, hearing and smell, and liquid for taste. So we should search[11] for a similar thing here (*i.e.* in the case of touch).

Themistius admits that air serves the like of all this. Since nothing can touch the fish[12] in the water without water as an intermediary, for moist cannot be wholely separated from the bodies in water, that which is in air is more reasonably not to be touched without air.

Sometimes, touch takes place through more than one medium, and even through that which is not natural, as happens when one's eye is covered, because one can apprehend hard, soft, hot and cold; or, for example, one can perceive with the help of a stick. But although perception is possible with the help of a stick we cannot perceive all kinds of the tangible, since through the stick we can feel neither hot nor cold, but we can only feel hard and soft. We touch hot and cold when the skin is covered, but this is not because the covering assists, but because it is affected and is sensed first.

But whether the sense of touch is flesh or in flesh, is not clear,[13] but whatever it may be, it is connected with flesh, and is one of those of which flesh is constituted.

The nature of the tangibles has been explained in many places. For this faculty has powers spread over the body[14] and their constitution is in the body in so far as it is a body. Hence, the sense of touch apprehends extensions and shapes, just as they are apprehended by sight.

As to the fact that there is no other sense beyond touch, this is clear by what we say: This is because if there were any other sense then it would have a particular sensible and this sensible must necessarily be a corporeal movent. There is, however, no corporeal movent except these five sensibles[15]. Hence, there cannot be a special sense organ for the common sensibles which will move several things. But the sense organ that apprehends them and how it works we shall soon explain later on. Again, if there were a sixth sense[16] a definite animal would necessarily have it, and this animal would necessarily be different from man, because man has only these five senses by nature, so this animal must be an imperfect animal. And it is absurd that the imperfect has got that which the perfect has not got. It has been shown in the first book of *the book on Animals*[17] how that which the imperfect animal has got resembles that which the perfect animal, namely, man, has not got, *e.g.* the lip of the ass and the trunk of the elephant and other limbs that characterise different animals although man has this in the most perfect way, for the broad lip and the trunk are imperfect hands. Since the limbs are defined only by their purposes, and are valued by their capacity to achieve those purposes—and these or what is better than these are in man—necessarily man should have this sense lest there be anything better than him. This is clear from what has been shown in the *book of Animals.*

CHAPTER IX

DISCOURSE ON COMMON SENSE

That all these senses are faculties for a single sense[1], which is the first and is called Common Sense, is clear by what we say : The existence of this faculty has been explained by what we wrote, in general, on Sense-perception, namely, this Common Sense is the matter through which the forms become sensible. Hence, whenever the forms become identical with one of the senses this sense is affected like matter when it is affected. So it is one in substratum and many in expression[2], as happens with the centre of a circle[3] which is one in substratum and many in expression.

Since there are many common sensibles, there should necessarily be a common faculty[4] to receive them. Hence, in touch and sight there is necessarily a single common faculty which receives that form.

What is this sense into which we inquire ? Again, there are then sensible things that are common to the five senses. So it is clear that there is a faculty common to them. This faculty passes judgment on the changing conditions of the sensible[5] and perceives its various states. For example, it perceives for every part of an apple[6] that it has taste, smell, colour, and warmth or cold; it decides that each of these is different from the other. Now if these states were in recipients that are contrary to this sense then it would not be possible for it to judge that " this " is other than " that "[7]. For it is necessary when the difference is observed to inquire into its nature.

In this faculty, the effects of the sensible things remain at the time when the sensible disappears, as happens to colours, because the function of this faculty is to cleave to the sensations which are the effects of the sensibles in it,[8] and when it has a chance to affect the sensible it perceives like the perception of effect. Hence, it is clear that the six faculties that are the "end" and the five that are the senses are souls, since these are entelechies of bodies. The seventh faculty is the moving faculty, we shall soon explain its nature later on.

But if there exists a faculty that does not employ an organ then it is not a soul except in the equivocal sense of the term. Since Common Sense is necessarily a form for the innate heat, it must necessarily be a soul. But it is not for this kind of relation that it is called soul, rather it is called so because it is an entelechy of the whole of the composite body. But it exists in the body only because it exists in its specific matter, and through it, in short, becomes a part of the body. And, it is through its being in the body that it is possible for the common sense to be connected with the senses and to be moved by the senses when they move that which is not corporeal. The common sense is not connected with that which is extraneous to the body.

The common sense becomes a form of the body which has organs, only by getting identified with the organs. It gets, for example, identified with eye. Hence a sleeping person does neither hear nor see. This is evident in those animals that do not close their eyes in sleep, since this form is not in the body. For that form is not separable from its matter, so when the body that has that form does not exist in the sense organ it is not perceived. The existence of that body in the sense organ is like the form of the sense organ, in the same way as the captain[9] is necessarily in the boat. The nature of this form has been explained elsewhere.

But when the common sense is alone,[10] then it is soul in so far as it is a form of a certain body. Hence, sleep is not found in all animals, since the innate heat belonging to the soul is in the sense organ only, because priority and posteriority in the soul is the same or the like, as has been shown in the *book of Animals*.

If, however, there is an animal which possesses another faculty that is not at all a form for a body, then this faculty is not soul except in the equivocal sense of the term. Take, for example, the case of the faculty that shows its existence when a body is present[11] to the common sense, and for which the common sense becomes like matter and the faculty the form for the matter of the common sense but not a first form. Hence, this faculty is an intermediary faculty between the soul and those faculties that are not souls but each of them derives its share from it, as we shall explain later on. This faculty is the faculty of imagination.

CHAPTER X

DISCOURSE ON THE FACULTY OF IMAGINATION

The imaginative faculty is the faculty by which the forms معانی of the sensibles[1] are apprehended. Some confusion is apparent in the study of those who have pondered over this faculty. Some hold that it is a sensation, others make it assumption[2]; others again judge that it is composed of opinion and sensation[3]. It is, however, clear that this faculty is neither one of the faculties of the soul nor is it composed of them[4]. For that which is true for one faculty of them in general is false for the part of the other, and is composed of a syllogism of the fourth class of the second figure, and a conclusion concerning the particular[5] third class is reached.

But the nature of an assumption is that it can be verified by the one who makes the assumption, while some imagination, formed by some one, can not be verified, for instance, to imagine that this horse has two horns—this cannot be assumed and its existence is not possible for the man who makes an assumption[6].

As for sensation, the sensible of every sensation exists[7] while it is perceived. But everything that is imagined is not like this[8], since sometimes one imagines things which have already ceased to be, and even things which cannot be perceived at all.

Nor is imagination composed of these two (*i.e.* opinion and sensation). This is evident by what we said about the nature of this faculty.

We say: That this is a faculty which apprehends only things that have been previously perceived—let us suppose, for instance, that the things are hidden from us either because they have perished, or because they do not get into the way of the receiver--is self-evident. This faculty is not possessed by man exclusively but it is in most irrational animals[9], for which there is no nobler faculty than this. We shall explain this later on.

This faculty can be true and false, but in most cases it is false[10]. When this faculty is true it necessarily apprehends by nature a thing in the same state in which it was perceived by sense-perception. It is obvious that the things apprehended by this faculty are not sensibles[11], this faculty only apprehends sensible things which have already vanished. Again, this faculty cannot apprehend essentially a sensible thing unless it has not been previously perceived by sense-perception, but accidentally. And how this happens has been summarised in *De Sensu* II[12]. It has already been stated before that sometimes a trace of the sensible thing remains in the common sense even after the sensible is not present in it[13]. But it is clear that this trace which is meant here is sensation, because, in addition to its faculty of receiving the form of the sensible thing, the common sense has the capacity of retaining[14] it ; and when through this faculty the form becomes actual, it appears to many people that they can see an individual without his being present[15]. This is clear in the case of "the pleuritics" (who have high temperature) to whom this happens in the state of waking[16], and it sometimes happens to certain temperaments that this is true[17], just as it happens to those who have "good sense-perception".

For when the common sense is strong and the natural disposition of the sense organ weak, the sense organ is acted upon by the common sense, and receives the impression and in its turn moves the compressed air which receives the impression and becomes like a phantom[18]. Next, the impression moves in its turn the sense organ, and the sense organ moves the common sense, as it is summarised in *De Sensu* II [19] where its cause has been demonstrated.

These sensations are the forms of the sensible things whose function, as explained in the chapter on Sense-perception, is to move the matter which is a recipient by nature. So when the forms become sensations and are separated[20] they are most apt for this. It is clear that matter in its existence is most akin to the common sense, and so it is moved by the sensations and perceives the forms of the sensible things. It is, however, not possible for the sensations themselves to be in the matter, because what is not divisible is not moved. Again, one thing that possesses matter cannot be matter for another thing except in so far as it moves another faculty which is its matter. As shown before, these kinds of matter are not the first matter but are different from it. But each of them is called matter equivocally. This is the imaginative faculty.

Representation is said either *per prius* or *per posterius*, and is said, in general, of the images of a thing. When it is said *per prius* it is said of the images of individual things. Sometimes it is said of the images of species, sometimes of an individual thing in a species in so far as it is the image of that species[21]. Hence,

Plato calls the sensible things images. Sometimes it is said of some other kinds. It is clear that the sensations are the representations of corporeal things through the faculty which apprehends these representations namely, the faculty of imagination. When these imaginations do not act in this faculty, nor do move it the animal cannot be moved by them, although it possesses mary movements in many ways. For an animal becomes warm and dry in so far as it consists of the elements, since being composed of elements it possesses quality[22]. It is potentially that it moves from place to place in so far as it is in space, and is altered by the passive faculty, and is acted upon by another passive faculty; and it sees through the visual faculty. Now some of these faculties are in the whole body, as *e g.* the faculty of being acted upon, and some in a particular limb, as *e.g.* the faculty of hearing. In the same way, again, it is moved by the imaginative faculty.

Since everything that is moved has a mover, the mover of this faculty is in the sensations that are in the common sense and it is this faculty which is moved. As to that through which things are imagined one after the other, and time after time, it is the far mover; and whether it is one or more than one has been discussed in *De Sensu* II[23]. Thus it is clear what the imaginative faculty is in general as well as what representation is

The images that are the entelechy of this faculty are in this faculty like the sensations in the common sense. It is evident that when the forms of the existents are images they are far more separated[24] from matter than the objects of sensation. The faculty of imagination is related to the faculty of sensation in this way but the faculty of imagination is not completely free from the immattered forms in so far as they are material; but it is in rank far from matter, since this faculty acts even if the immattered forms are not present, but in its being it needs them by necessity. If an image, however, exists without the immattered forms then it is of a different kind and its nature has been explained in many places.

The faculty of imagination is not moved unless it is set in motion by sensations[25], and when there is no sensation this faculty is not set in motion. When there is no sensation of this kind this faculty has nothing to act upon, and hence, this faculty suffers transformation—if transformation[26] can be said of that which is indivisible—from one thing to another thing. How this happens has been explained in *De Sensu II.* Hence, when the common sense is occupied or when we assume that it has disappeared it is not acted upon by the imaginative faculty but remains pure potentiality, just as it is assumed that this happens when a man perceives dreadful things in darkness[27]. This is why the imaginative faculty has been listed among the material faculties, and hence, its action in sleep[28] is most apparent, for sleep is nothing but the mere potential existence of the common sense. It preserves in sleep, however, the existents that occur but is not moved by them and is only moving, and the imaginative faculty is moved by it alone. But in a waking, condition, when the common sense perceives strong sensations[29], it seems only moved ; and at that time it is either eclipsed or remains mere potentiality, its movement in potentiality not being observed. This has been summarized in many places. Hence, when the senses are of no avail the faculty of common sense is of no avail, and when the common sense is of no avail the faculty of imagination is of no avail. This is why this faculty perishes when the common sense perishes; and it exists while it depends upon the common sense, just as the moved depends upon the mover in the state in which it sets it in motion. But in its being this faculty is nobler than the common sense, since it is like the end for it.

It is through this faculty that animals move in various ways and the appetitive part[30] is moved; and through it animals have many arts and crafts, and look after their progeny, as for instance, ants and bees[31].

This faculty is the most noble in irrational animals; and in irrational animals there is no other moving faculty more perfect than this faculty. For the moving faculties that are in animals by nature are the nutritive and sensitive faculties; and through all these they perform those actions which are said to be essentially from them, since mover and moved are together in them, as has been explained in Physics VIII.[32]

Now it is clear that the imaginative faculty is an entelechy for a natural organised body, and so it is soul. It is obvious from what we said that there cannot be any other faculty besides these two, I mean the common sense and the faculty of imagination. This is because the existents are either material or separated from matter. The material existents are in a specific body. And, separation is a movement, and every movement is a change or dependent on change.[33] Separation, however, depends upon change, and the dependent is either primary or secondary. As shown before, the first is sensation, and the second is this (*i.e.* imagination). If there were a third thing then there must necessarily be in the substratum a state through which the second could be distinguished from the third, since both together were from a single genus, otherwise what would make the second different from the third?

There (*i e.* in the case of the common sense) the movement is in matter and here (*i.e.* in imagination) the movement is not in the matter of the species, while the secondaries are contrary to those species that are not in matter But that which is not in matter is said in many ways : either (a) it cannot be in matter so as to demonstrate the existence of a thing that is of this description, or (b) it may have matter but is considered in a state in which it is contrary to matter, and it is in this state that it is what it is and is considered with the being that characterises it—this is the reasoning, as we shall soon explain—or (c) it is that which is in matter, but is taken in so far it is what it is. This is because of the alternative that separation is either possible in it—this is the common sense—or that it is separated, but is taken in the state in which it is in matter—this is the representing faculty of imagination. Hence, the faculty of representation apprehends the individuals[34] only, since the immattered forms move these faculties only through the faculty that is in them, namely, the faculty whose nature has already been explained before this.[35] Thus, the sensations are generated while they possess a faculty through which they cause motion, and so they move the imaginative faculty and the images come to be. All this happens through forms that are material but are different from the immattered forms.[36] But in these forms the percipient faculty is unable to move the 'universal'[37] form unless these specific immattered forms move that which is moved by the whole of the specific lest this faculty of imagination would move indefinitely, since movement is caused by a being that is connected with finiteness. That which is moved through matter and finiteness is matter in so far as it is matter; and the separable existent moves with an infinite movement only in so far as it is not moved. But as there is no contrary here so there is no separation here. If matter were a recipient eternally the separable body would have been mover eternally, because if it were not to move then it would suffer motion; and everything moved is divisible, and everything divisible is material. Hence, the faculty of imagination apprehends those states of the immattered forms that characterise them at the time when it apprehends them; and it does not perceive those states which do not characterize them at the time of perception. It is, however, not possible for it to perceive the immattered forms with all their states that qualify the form due to the properties that are separable from it. Hence, the imaginative faculty apprehends all their essential and non-essential qualities as a single thing.

But a questionner may ask and say: "How can a single thing be apprehended in its various states, some of which are apprehended and some are not apprehended in it ; but, indeed, some of them are possible in it, and others not ? But this is in man only, because it is he who synthesizes and analyzes.[38] This motion is caused by other causes which have been enumerated in the second book of Aristotle's book on Sensation.[39]

If the faculty of imagination were to apprehend the 'form' and what can be apprehended of it, then this would be possible in the speculative mind But in assumption it is a thing that is possible indeed ; and we shall soon explain assumption and its faculty. It is then clear what the rational faculty is. But, in knowledge, it (*i.e.* contemplation of the meaning and its apprehension) is the activity of the reasoning faculty, and sometimes, of course, it is not at all possible in it ; and we shall soon explain why it is so later on.

The faculty of imagination is, therefore, like a sweet fragrance between the existents whose nature is to be separated from matter and those that are material, and takes from each a share in the same way as Nature acts eternally, for, as has been shown in many places, it never changes from one genus to another genus without a medium. This is the last of that which is moved by the specific sensible.

As shown elsewhere, everything moved is homogeneous to the mover, and the image is particular, and not universal which is the opposite extreme of the particular. But these two faculties (*i.e.* those of reasoning and imagination) are no via media in the same way as there are media in heat and cold, so that they would be in sense-perception. Representation is a part of the universal, as this is so in that which is between heat and cold; and the medium contains heat and cold. For there is neither in sensation nor in representation anything universal, but sensation and representations have states in which they become nearer to each other. These states are most frequent in and suitable for thoughts,[40] but they are more manifest in sensations. For the particular is not contrary to the universal, but it is somehow different from it; Aristotle has explained its nature in the *Metaphysics*.[41]

As to the existence of the universal, it is necessarily due to some other reasons, and is either 'becoming' or 'not-becoming'. If it is becoming then there is matter in it, or a potentiality like matter; if it is not becoming so that learning would be recollection then it follows that it must either belong to the forms, as held by Plato—this is what has been recorded by Socrates in the *Phaedo*[42]—and so it belongs to mind like sensation or something homogeneous to it, or it must belong to mind before it understands it, and 'learning' will then be recollection.

When the universal is studied it is found in certain states from which it follows that it is eternal, and in certain other states from which it follows necessarily that it is generated. In short, its necessary properties that are found in it are in a state that opposes their existence in the immattered forms. Whatever be the nature of their existence in the immattered forms, and whatever be the nature of the universal, the being of its properties is contrary to the material being with a very clear contrariety. And the most conceivable with them is to be with a different kind of existence so that existence would be predicated of them and of the material existent equivocally. The most reasonable with existence is that it is predicated of the properties *per prius* although the universal is the most suitable for existence.

CHAPTER XI

DISCOURSE ON THE REASONING FACULTY

It is necessary for us to inquire into the reasoning faculty as to what faculty it is, what its nature is, and whether it is soul or a faculty of a soul. If it is a faculty of a soul, as is assumed, then in what respect is it related to the soul? We must investigate whether this faculty is always actuality[1] or sometimes potentiality and sometimes actuality. If the second alternative is true then it must possess matter, and if it has matter then it has a mover, since everything moved has a mover. Now, what is this mover[2] and what is its nature? With all these (questions) agrees what is commonly known about this faculty, and about those states of the physical body that are observed by sense-perception. For this will give the inquirer things that are said in this connection; this information about all these questions will itself direct him to the soul properly.

That this faculty is not always in actuality is clear, because if it were so then 'learning' must be 'recollection[3]' and learning would certainly not depend upon sense-perception,[4] and it would not have been that when we are deficient in a particular sense we would be deficient in a particular science. But the matter is different.[5] And then it would have been through this faculty that the knowledge about the existence of things that are depending on the sensible would have been gained without having recourse to sense-perception. Hence, the man who has, for instance, not perceived weight will have certain knowledge of all its attributes the certainty of which is generally attained by the man who perceives it with his senses. This is obvious, and to prolong the discussion about it is superfluous. Moreover, this has been explained in many places.

That this faculty is always potential is also absurd, since man acquires sciences either by sense-perception, as is the case with the people of the practical arts and crafts or by learning.

This faculty is therefore sometimes potential and sometimes actual. The transition from potentiality to actuality is a change, and so there must be one who causes change, since all that is moved has a mover, as we have shown before.

It is through the reasoning faculty that a man perceives another man to be alike to himself in accordance to what presents itself to his soul[6]. In short, 'logos' is either a statement, or an inquiry, or a commandment. Inquiry is to seek information, and giving information is teaching and inquiry is learning. Now, it is through this faculty that man teaches or learns. These three parts exist only when man is in his natural state. Consequently, to speak certain words makes by convention recur to the soul all those meanings that are understood by the speaker. 'Logos' (النطق) in the language of the Arabs indicates first to utter words that indicates meanings. Next, it is used for uttering sounds which may not indicate any meaning. Hence, a poet says:

"Nothing prevented her (the she-camel) from drinking except that a dove cooed (literally: 'spoke') amidst the branches bearing fruits (of palm-tree)."[7]

Sometimes they use "logos" for something else, as has been discussed by the lexicographers in their language.

Since this is so that this faculty has an organ which is, as we described its activity before, the most suitable for speech, those who philosophise transferred this term to this organ. We have already described the faculty which is the object of this discourse Now, we intend to explain its nature and origin, because the investigation of the ancients was concerning this only, and that whether it is aqueous (?)[8] or not aqueous. It is not difficult for one who intends to enumerate the views held by the predecessors, because all are well-known. This is why we drop from our discussion the enumeration and examination of these views, and we restrict ourselves to what necessarily follows from what man naturally knows about it, because the views expressed about this faculty are not of this kind ; they are indeed mere conjectures most of which, according to those who held them, are either some assumptions or well-known opinions. An investigation of these views either gives the information of its nature according to a certain state, or makes a man stop at the place of error committed by those who held them. This is a kind of dialectic exercise.

We, therefore, say: It is a self-evident fact that informing and transforming happen only through a proposition[9], and what decision is has been explained in the *Peri Hermenias*, and that it is composed of a predicate and a subject. Thus in man there are necessarily two actions : one the existence of "separate notions", the other, the synthesis of these two notions. The faculty through which this synthesis takes place is the thinking faculty, its function being the different modes of composing the separate meanings[10], which I have explained in the books on Logic. The second faculty is that through which the separate meanings are determined. This (*i e.* the latter) is like matter for the former. For when the separate meanings are not found the composition is not possible. So the latter is prior to the former by nature.

As enumerated in many places, the meanings indicated by words are of two kinds[11]: universals and particulars. As shown before, the faculty by which the particulars are perceived is the imaginative faculty. But the universals belong to another faculty[12]. It is clear that they do not belong to sense-perception, and that the sense-perception perceives the particulars only. The universals have different meanings, since the universal is a particular notion from the rest of that which is predicated of the many; the case is not so for the two particulars, since every premiss is to be composed of two particulars, and so it is rare in use; we shall speak of it afterwards. But the premiss composed of one particular and one universal is often found in "soothsaying", in rhetoric and in verse. As to the premiss that is composed of two universals, it is common to all arts and is called sciences in general and *per prius.* Now, then, that which has a principle like this is rational at least in potentiality, and it is in this way that "rational" is said of man.

These universals are intelligible meanings and are universals[13] only through their relation to the particulars that are formed for them; similar is the meaning of the sun and the moon. In short, those that have only one individual are intelligible meanings, and are universals only in an analogous way, and they are called universals *per posterius.*

These intelligibles are either eternal or accidental.

Here ends what exists from his discourse (on the Soul). May Allah show him Mercy !

NOTES

INTRODUCTION

(1) See Ibn al-'Imām's preface to the MS. also quoted by Ibn Abī 'Uṣaibi'ah in his 'Uyūn al-'Anbā', ed. Müller, vol. ii, p. 63; Ibn Ṭufayl : Ḥayy Ibn Yaqẓān, ed. Gauthier, p. 12.

(2) For the biography of Ibn Bājjah see Brockelmann: Geschichte, vol. i, p. 601, Supl. i. 830 ; E. of Islam, ii, 366 ; Sarton : Int. History of Science, i, vol. i, p. 183.

(3) Cf. JRAS, 1945, p. 62.

(4) For his biography see Ibn 'Abi 'Uṣaibi'ah : 'Uyūn al-'Anbā', ed. Müller, vol. II, p. 63.

(5) Cf. the Bodl. MS Poc. 206, Fol. 4A : وكتاب النفس ينقص منه مقدار يسير ذكر الوزير انه سقط منه بعد وقوعه اليه , also Fol. 120B : وكتاب النفس ينقص منه مقدار يسير ذكر الوزير سقط منه بعد وقوعه اليه .

(6) Ḥayy Ibn Yadzān, ed. Gauthier, p. 12-13.

(7) See the Bodl. MS. Poc. 206, Fol. 113B27 : كتبناه في كتاب النفس ; Fol. 220A18 : و قد لخصنافي كتابنا في النفس ; about other works see, for example, Fol. 89A24 : كتبناها في شرح الرابعة من الآثار

(8) Cf. Ibn Khaldūn : Tārīkh, vol. i Bulaq, p. 519 ; Maqqari : Nafḥ al-Ṭib, vol. iv, pp. 201-206 ; Sarton : Introduction of the History of Science, vol. i, p. 183.

(9) See page 3.

(10) See al-Andalūs, 1942, p. 22-23 ; Al-Ahwāni's edition of T.K. al-Nafs li 'Ibn Rushd, p. 117 : اثبت هذا القول في زمان منفصل بالداخل الى والخارج عنى فلما قرأته رأيت فيه تقصيرا عن افهام ما كنت اردت افهامه، فان المعنى المقصود برهان ليس يعطيه هذاالقول اعطاء بينا الا بعدا عسرواستكراه شديد . . . وكذلك وجدت ترتيب العبارة في بعض مواضع على غيرالريق الاكمل ولم يلتسع الوقت لتبديلها . . .

(11) Cf. the Bodl. MS Fol. 120B قال القاضي الحسن بن محمد بن محمد بن محمد بن النضر وهوالمعروف بالاديب

(12) Ḥayy Ibn Yaqẓān, ed. Gautier, p. 13.

(13) Ed. al-Ahwāni, p. 90, ed. Hyderabad, omits this portion.

(14) See Rasā'il Ibn Rushd, Hyderabad. 1946, p. 110.

(15) Cf. Ibnal-Nadīm : al-Fihrist, ed, Flügel, Leipzig, vol. i, p. 251 ; al-Qifṭi : Tārīkh al-Ḥukamā', ed. Lippert, p. 41.

(16) Al-Qifṭi : Tārīkh al-Ḥukamā, ed. Lippert, p. 279.

(17) Ed. Flügel, p. 251.

(18) Al-Qifṭi : Tārīkh, p. 54.

(19) Ibid., p. 257.

(20) The Bodl. MS. ous. 95.· fol. 41B-52B, the Colophon is as follows : تمام شد مقاله سیوم و بتمامی آن کتاب نفس منسوب بارسطا طالیس در وقت غروب خورشید روز یکشنبه در بام مسجد حضرت امام حسن عسکری که در پهلوی روضه فاطمه بنت موسی کاظم (علیها السلام) است و رقم بتاریخ شهر جمادی الثانی سنه ١٦٣٩ھ والحمد لله رب العالمین اولا و آخر او ظاهرا و باطنا والصلوة علی سید الانبیاء و قدوة الاصفیاء و علی افضل الاوصیا وسفخر اولاولیاء

(21) Also quoted by Ibn Abi 'Uṣaibi'ah, ed. Müller, ii, 63.

(22) See page 7 : والخمس التی هی الحواس بین من امرها انها انفس

(23) Cf. page 7 : والسابعة هی القوة المحرکة

(24) See the Bodl. MS. Fol. 129B : والنفس النزوعیة اما ان یکون جنسالثلاث قوی وهی النزوعیة بالخیال وبها یکون التربیة للاو لاد و التحرک اشخاص المکان والالف والعشق وما یجری مجراه والنفس النزوعیة بالنفس المتوسطة وبها تشتاق الغذاء والدیار وجمیع الصنایع داخلة فی هذه وهاتان مشترکتان للحیوان ومنها النزوعیة التی تشعربالنطق وبها یکون التعلیم وهذه یختص بها الانسان فقط

(25) Fuṣūṣ ed. Dieterici, Al-Farābis Philosophical Abhandlungen, 73, 74. Khalil Geor, in his article published in the Journal Revue des Etudes Islamique, 1941-46, pp. 31-39, has shown that the book is wrongly attributed to al-Farābi ; it is really a work of Ibn Sīnā.

(26) Shifa', Bodl. MS. foll. 161A, 182A, 183; F. Raḥman : Avicenna's Psychology.

(27) Cf. page 7 :

(28) The Bodl. MS. Fol. 220B : فان النفس الفاعلة و ذالک لان النفس تقال علی سخوینا کما تلخص فیما کتبناه فی النفس فالنفس اذا قیلت علی الکمال الاول کانت قوة منفعلة واذا قیلت علی الکمال الاخیر کانت قوة فاعلة ـ

(29) The Bodl. MS. Fol. 136B : و رأی بقوتة الناطقة حین فاضت علیها الموهبة تلک المهبة کماتری بقوة العین ضوءالشمس بضوءالشمس والسبب القریب فی ادراک المعقولات وحصول القوة الناطقة بالفعل هوالموهبة التی هی مثل ضوءالشمس زمیصربها ویری مخلوقات الله تعالی حتی یکون من یوسن بالله ملائکة وکعبة الخ والتفاضل فی موهبة الله التی بها بتصرالقوة الناطقه متقارن بحسب ما یعطیه الله : Fol. 137A ایضافی اول خاقه الانسان من الاستعدادلقبول الموهبة التی بها تبصر القوة الناطقة

(30) Ibid. Fol. 136B : وبرى مخلوقات الله تعالى حتى يكون . . . كتبه ورسا ورسله والرار الاخرة ايمانا يقينا فيكون من الذين يذكرون الله وياما وقعودا وعلى جنوبهم ويتفكرون فى خلق السماو ان والارض و اختلاف الليل والنهار ولا فكرة الا بتلك الموهبة' وتلك الموهبة هي الصتاله 'بالعقل الفعال

(31) Cf. Foll. 123b, 124b, 125a.

(32) See Ibn Khallikān, ed. Wustenfeld, vol. 1-7, no. 681 (1835).

(33) Cf. The article of Mr. Dunlop, JRAS, 1945, p. 62.

(34) Cf. al-Andalus, 1940, '42, '43.

(35) For example, the Berlin MS. omits النزوعية which is inserted in the margin in the Oxford MS. See al-Andalus, 1942, p. 12 (رسالة الاتصال). For other examples see Al-Andalus, vol. 5 1940 pp. 266-278, كتاب النبات.

(36) For example, القوة المنميه is read by Prof. Asin Palacios as 'القوة المتمنية' ; see al-Andalus, vol. 7, 1942, p. 12; also 1940, p. 267: و فان كان للنبات ذكر وانثى فاعنما يحب ان يكون ذلک فى التميزة فقط' فاما ما ليس بمتميز... I would read المثمرة, and بمثمر respectively. The Oxford MS. says المتميزة and بمتمر .

(37) For example, see al-Andalus, 1942, p. 12, last line : فانما يكون حينئذ انسانا بالقوة , the Oxford MS. reads بالقوة الفكرية (Fol. 216B); 1943, p. 37 : . . . و ذلک فى السار فتكون كالحالم the MS. reads فيكون كمالک كالحالم , p. 40 : اذ هو منقسم , MS. اذ هو جسم منقسم .

(38) Cf. JRAS, 1945, p. 6.

(39) Cf. Cairo, 1905, p. 8 ft.

(40) Oxford, 1671, p. A2.

NOTES

CHAPTER I

(ON THE SOUL)

In this chapter Ibn Bājjah treats the nature of the soul and its definition, discusses the excellence of psychology, emphasizes that out of the three Aristotelian methods of describing things—namely, the method of division, the method of composition, and the syllogistic method—the method of composition alone has to be used for defining this science, and suggests that the souls of all animals should be studied, forms of plants being yet a problem to be investigated.

Ibn Bājjah like Aristotle bases his psychology on physics. He begins his discussion of the soul and its definition by stating that bodies, natural or artificial, are composed of matter and form, form being the permanent acquisition or the entelechy of the body.

Entelechy is of various kinds. For it belongs either to those existents that perform their actions without being essentially moved, or to those that act while they are being acted upon.

A natural body is composed of both mover and moved, whereas the artificial body has its mover outside. Now the form that supplies the entelechy of a natural body without organs is called Nature, and the one that supplies the entelechy of a natural body which is moved through an organ is called Soul. The soul is, therefore, defined as the first entelechy in a natural organized body.

But because " entelechy " is an ambiguous term the term " soul " is also ambiguous. Ibn Bājjah, therefore, defines the nutritive, the sensitive and the imaginative soul as the entelechy of the nutrient, the sentient, and the imaginative organic body respectively.

Psychology is the most excellent science, and precedes all natural and mathematical sciences. Even Metaphysics cannot be studied without knowing soul and intellect. Knowledge of a thing has, however, several relations, namely, knowledge of the quiddity of the thing, knowledge of its particular essential qualities. We must, therefore, investigate whether the soul is one or not, whether it has parts or not, whether it has several faculties or only one faculty; Democritus, the atomists, Galen, Plato and other ancient philosophers having maintained the one or the other of these views.

But the ancient philosophers who preceded Aristotle had confined their study to the human soul alone, whereas the knowledge of the soul of every animal is a part of natural science.

As said before, soul is an equivocal term, because it is not a single nature. If it were homogeneous in nature its functions would have likewise been homogeneous. Sense-perception, for example, precedes the imaginative soul, the faculty of sensation is preceded by the faculty of nutrition, and the rational faculty comes last of all ; indeed the perfect comes by nature after the imperfect.

Hence, all kinds of soul cannot be defined in one and the same way.

(1) See Ibn Bājjah, the Majmu'ah, Fol. [187a : قال اُرسطو ان الموجودات منها ما هی بالطبیعه، ومنها من قبل اسباب اخرعدة، اولاها من قبل الطبیعه . . . وقوله "ما وجودها باسباب اخر" ولم یقل "المهنه" لان من الاجسام ما هی موجودة بالمهنه و تلک مشهورة، و منها ما هی موجودة عن اصناف الحیوان غیرالناطق، وبین ان قواها لیس مهنا فان قیل لها مهن فبالاستعارة کالعسل والشمع الموجودین عن النحل cf. Arist. : Physics iii, 192b8 ; Al-Fārābi : Iḥṣā'ul-'Ulūm, p. 45, Madrid, 1932. ; also Fuṣūl al-Madani (the Bodl. MS. Hunt 307), Fol. 92b : الاجسام منها صناعیة ومنها طبیعیة والصناعیة مثل السریر والسیف والزجاج واشباه ذلک، والطبیعیة مثل الانسان وسایرالحیوانات Ibn Rushd : Raṣā'il, Hyderabad, 1947, p.12.

(2) The products of art, e.g. chair, bedstead and the like, have no principle of movement and rest in themselves. They are incidentally manufactured. Vide Ibn Bāj. Fol. 92a : . . . فان السریر لایتحرک بما هو سریر اصلا، ولا ایضا یتحرک الخشب بقوة فیه الی ان یصیر سریرا و لایتحرک بقوة یفیده ایاها السریر الی ان یکون سریرا ولا یتحرک الخشب ایضا بقوة یفیده ایاها شی اخر بل انما یتحرک ما دام المحرک له موجودا وهو متناه وهذ المحرک هو صناعة ولیست بطبیعة

Cf. Arist. Phys. ii, I. 192b15-25.

(3) Natural things are all transitory. Vide Ibn Baj. Fol 6b : . . . الاجسام الطبیعیة اما ان تکون کلها کاینة فاسدة علی ما نشاهد فی کل مانحسه

Cf. Arist. Phys. ii. 1. 192b9-14.

(4) The expression العاسية is found in the writings of Al-Fārābi (see Masā'il Mutafarriqa, Hyderabad, p.6 ; Al Fārā-bi's Philosophische Abhandlungen, p. 87, ed. Dieterici : سئل عن الاشياء العاسية), in the translations of Ḥunayn, Ibn Isḥāq (see K. Ṭimā'ūs, p. 19 : الام العاسية, published by Paul Kraus and R. Walzer under the title, " Galeni Compendium Timaei Platonis "). Ibn Bājja. obviously after al-Fārābi has repeatedly used this expression ; see Fol. 187b : و هذه هى الامور العاسية على الاطلاق للطبيعة also Fol. 169a ... وما العاسية فهى : (or Tadbir. p. 21, ed. Asin Palacios). But al-Kindi (see Rasā'il al-Kindi al-Falsafiyah, ed. Abū Rīda, p. 382), Ibn Sinā' (see Shifa, the Bodl. MS. Pocock 125, Fol. 23a3) and Ibn Rushd (see al-Samā', Rasā'il, Hyd., pp. 5 and 21.) preferably use العامة .

(5) Ibn Bājjah in al-Samā', Fol. 5b writes : ولما شرع فى هذا الفحص من النظر وجد رسومها (الطبيعة) قريب المأخذ من العلوم المتعارفة ، و وجد العلم بوجودها فى الثلاثة التى هى المادة و الصورة و الفاعل بينا . . . اما فى الاجسام الصناعية فظاهر ، و اما فى الطبيعية ففى بعضها يظهر نحواما من الظهور و فى بعضها يخفى كل الخفاء Cf. Arist. Phys. i. 7. 190b20.

(6) Cf. The Ar. Text infra; Fol. 153A, p. 91 Damascus.

(7) Ibn Bajj in al-Sama', Fol. 7a, argues that if matter is not formless then it will be divided in "matter" and "form", and this will go on *ad infinitum* : فانا متى وضعنا المادة ذات صورة لزم ان تكون منقسمة الى مادة و صورة و يمر ذلك الى غير نهاية . . . و هذا أيضا شنيع. بل محال Cf. Arist. Phys. i. 7. 191 a 8. فستنتهى ضرورة الى مادة غير ذات صورة.

(8) Cf. Arist. De Caelo, iii. 1. 298a 29.

(9) By the expression جسم طبيعى Ibn Bājja means " a body composed of matter and form ", see al-Samā', Fol. 8a : ... بوجوده الجسم الطبيعى، و وجوده يتم بوجود المادة و الصورة و كلواحد منهما طبيعة . . . . فالطبيعة اخلق بالصورة من المادة ، الا انها لما لم تكن دون المادة لم توجد بالفعل ، فالمادة معاضدة لها ، فالمادة ايضا طبيعة و المجتمع منهما هوالجسم الطبيعى .

Aristotle calls the four elements " elementary natural bodies ", vide Phys. iv. 1. 208b 8.

(10) Ibn Bājjah differentiates between the change that occurs in the form of a body, which he calls تكون , genesis (vide the Text) and change that takes place in the differentia, which he names استحاله, alteration (vide al-Sama ', Fol. 16b :والحركة في الكيف يقال لها استحالة ; and also the Ar. Text). He further explains in Al-Kawn wa'l-Fasād, Fol. 80b. that, according to those who hold that the existing thing is one, تكون, genesis, is necessarily استحاله, alteration, but according to others who believe that it is more than one in species, تكون is necessarily not استحاله ; (و بالجملة ، فمن جعل الموجود واحدا فهو يرى ضرورة ان التكون استحالة . . . و اما من جعل الموجود اكثر من واحد بالنوع . . . فهو يضع بالضرورة ان التكون غير الاستحالة) .

(11) Cf. Arist. Phys. i. 7. 190b 18.

(12) This is based on what Aristotle says : " For the helmsman knows and prescribes what sort of form a helm should have, the other from what wood it should be made and by means of what operations. In the products of art, however, we make the material with a view to the function, whereas in the products of nature the matter is there all along" ; see Phys. ii. 2. 194 b 5.

(13) As Ibn Bājjah explains, the first mover is of various kinds : (i) that which moves without being moved, e.g. ice which makes the pot cold but itself is not affected by cold; (ii) that which moves and is only accidentlly moved, e.g. art ; (iii) that which moves and is not moved neither essentially nor accidentally ; cf. Al-Samā'', Fol. 32 b : والمحرک الاول يقال على انحاء : احدها المحرک الذی يحرک لا بان يتحرک کالثلج' يبرد الاناء لا بانه يتبرد' فان الثلج 'يبرد الاناء و الاناء يبرد الماء' و الاناء يبرد و يتبرد معا و الثلج يبرد ولايتبرد' و قد يقال على ما يحرک و هو لا يتحرک و لا يمکن فيه ان يتحرک الا بالعرض' و قد يقال على ما يحرک و لا يتحرک لا بالذات و لا بالعرض 'فظاهر ان القول الاول حدلانه بين الوجود ' و اما الثانی فانه ايضا يتبين انه معنى موجود فان الصناعة تحرک و لا تتحرک ولا يمکن ان تتحرک الابالعرض -

(14) The source of this division of ' mover ' is in Aristotle's Physics, viii. 5. 256 a 6 : " Either the movent is not

itself responsible for the motion, which is to be referred to something else which moves the movent, or the movent is itself responsible for the motion. Further, in the latter case, either the movent immediately precedes the last thing in the series, or there may be one or more intermediate links . . . ".

Ibn Bājjah repeatedly refers to this division in his al-Sama' as follows Fol. 56b : (ای من المحرک) (a) و منه
بالذات كاليد التى تحرک العكاز، و منه (b) بالعرض فان الابيض يحرک
العكاز ؛ وما بالذات فهی ضرورة متناهية كما بين ذلک فی السابعة من هذا
الكتاب والمحرک الاول هو الابعد؛ فان الا بعد يحرک منفردا بنفسه؛ و
اما المتوسطات فكلها انما تحرک بالابعد فابعد ؛ والابعد هو المحرک
الاول (منها : b. MS. منها , a. MS.) والمحرک :
Fol. 50 a : ان المحرک و المتحرک بعضها بطريق العرض. المحركة بذاتها
fol. 48a : ينفصل بتقابل يخصه و هو ان يحرک بنفسه . . . و قد يحرک
بغيره . Cf. De Gen. i. 7.324 a 30 sq.

That which has no soul can only move by being connected with a mover. It is actually a thing moved and is being acted upon; (Ibn Bājjah, al-Samā', Fol. 50a :
ان كل ما ليس بذی نفس فليس محركا بل هو متحرک منفعل، و انما هو
محرک باقتران المحرک به.)

(16) The last mover is that which is connected with the thing moved in the same way as an agent is in contact with the object acted upon ; al-Samā ', Fol. 36a : و قد ثبت فی
اقاويلنا فی الكون والفساد البرهان على ان الفاعل يلي المنفعل و يماسه، و بمثل
ذلک بعينه يمكن ان يبين ان المحرک يلي المتحرک والذی زيدهنا ان المحرک
القريب عند al-Kawn ; Fol. 81b : فالمحرک اذا حرک المتحرک
فقد ماس هذا المحرک ز بطبيعة ذلک المتحرک و المتحرک محسوس
ان كل متحرک فهو يتلوا : Fol. 82b محركه الاقرب . . . فالمتحرک
و المحرک يتماسان.

Cf. Arist. Phys. vii.2.243 a 3.

(17) The wood, for example, has no capacity to become a couch, nor can it get any capacity to become couch from the couch itself or its like. But it is moved so long as a mover moves it, and this mover is art and not nature; cf. Ibn Bāj. al-Ḥayawān. Fol. 92a (see supra note 2).

(18) Motion actually takes place by the first mover which is not moved by the last mover, and is, therefore, responsible for the movement ; Ibn Baj. al-Samā', Fol. 50 a :فان الانسان يحرک اليد و اليد العکاز والعکاز يحرک الحجر، والمحرک الاول هوالانسان و اليه ينسب الفعل فى الحقيقة و هوالمستحق للذم والمدح والعقاب والثواب).

Cf. Arist. Phys. viii. 5. 256 a 9.

(19) Cf. Arist. Phys. viii. 4. 254 b 14 ; ii.1.193 a 29.

(20) As stated above (اما الصناعة فانها لا تحرک بذاتها), art does not move essentially, but it moves through instruments. Ibn Bājjah explains the phrase بالقصد الثانى by saying, that when a man, for example, intends to fight his enemy, he not only intends to fight the enemy : but also those who come to help the enemy. His intention of fighting with the helpers is, therefore, a second intention, the first being the 'intention of fighting with the enemy' ; (al-Samā', Fol. 9a : فان انسانا اذا قصد انسانا ليحاربه فقد قصد ليحارب من يعاونه لکن بالقصد الثانى لا بالاول .)

Art, however, causes change and completes what nature leaves unfinished ; cf. Arist. Phys. ii.2.194 a 36 ; ii, 8. 199 a 15.

(21) The difference between artificial forms, though existent in matter, have no capacity to move anything else, nor can they move that which contains them. But the natural forms are movers, and possess the power of moving other bodies ; (Ibn Bāj. al-Ḥayawān, Fol. 92b : و ليس للصورالصناعية و هى الموجودة فى موادها، قوة على ان تحرک ماهى فيه و لا على ان تحرک غيرها، و هذا هوالفرق بين الصور الصناعية و بين الطبيعية ، فان الصور الطبيعية، فيها قوى يحرک بها الاجسام و يتحرک بهاالاجسام ايضا على انها المحرکة).

Cf. Arist. Phys. ii.1.193 a 30-65.

(22) Ibn Bājjah describes کمال as follows : "Some existing things are either bodies or in bodies. In so far as they are bodies, they are determined by nature, e.g. man and horse. But some of these bodies are determined by accident and have in themselves no size to characterise them.

Now nothing of the first group can exist in part, since if there is no perfection there is no being. This perfection or entelechy like كون (generation) and فساد (corruption) is no movement but a change which does not occur in substance, and so the one that suffers this change remains the same. This change is called 'entelechy' when it is from 'not-being' to 'being' like the change from جهل (ignorance or not-knowing) to علم (knowing). Aristotle has not given attention to this distinction between 'entelechy' and 'movement', and treats them alike, whereas 'movement' is that which is for, to or from 'the being with entelechy'; cf. al-Samā', Fol. 15b : ومن الموجودات التى هى اجسام او فى اجسام من جهة انها اجسام ما هى محدودة بالطبع كالانسان والفرس، و منها ما هى محدودة بعرض وليس لها فىانفسها قدر يخصها فالاول لايمكن ان يوجد فيه شيئى بجزءه لان الكمال متى لم يوجد لم يكن ذلك الوجود. واماالذى يبقىفيه المتغير واحدا ; Fol. 16a;

بعينه فظاهران التغير لا يكون فى الجوهر فان كان من عدم الى وجود كالتغير من الجهل

الى العلم سمى استكمالا فالكون والفساد ليسا بحركتين ; Fol 16b : وكذلك الاستكمال وهذا ما لم يلتفته ارسطو بل اجراه مجرى الحركة فى مكان اخر، فالحركة اذا هى لموجود بالكمال ومن وجود بالكمال

والى موجود بالكمال:Aristotle usually calls motion the entelechy of matter, the soul the entelechy of the body; cf. Phys. iii. I. 201a 10, b4; 2.202 b7; viii. I, 251a 9; Met. xi. 9.1065 b 16, 33.

(23) Ibn Bājjah also speaks of the grades of 'entelechy' in Al-Samā ' Fol. 52b : "The existence of a thing in space is a kind of entelechy which is of various grades : (i) the lowest of all is that which is only in one place where it remains till it perishes ; (ii) next being that which moves in its place in different times and is always actual and potential ; (iii) third stage being that in which it is moved due to connection ; (فان وجود الشيئى فى المكان جنس من اجناس الكمال و هو على مراتب : فاقلها ان يكون فى موضع واحد فقط ولا يبارحه حق يفسد ، ثم من بعد ذلك ان يتحرك حتى يكون فى جميع تلك المواضع فى زمان زمان فيكون ابدا بالفعل و بالقوة، والمرتبة الثالثة ان يتحرك فيها على الاتصال) -

(24) Cf. Ibn Baj. Fol. 130a : وقد تبين فى الثامنة ان كل متحرك فله محرك

(25) In al-Samā', Fol. 32b, Ibn Bājjah says: "Some products of art like automatic machines, have their mover inside; and as it is not manifest to our senses, we wonder when we see them moving by themselves ; (فان هذه الميكانات والاشياء الصناعية التى يخفى محركها يظهر للحس انها تتحرك من قبلها فيقع العجب منها' See also Fol. 130a: وهذا (المحرك) قد يكون طبيعيا و بذاته وهو كاصناف الحيوان وقد يكون صناعيا كالميكانة .

Aristotle refers to 'automatic machines', vide De Gen. An. ii. I. 734 b 10; 'catapults', vide Politics, 1331a.

(26) Evidently Ibn Bājjah refers to his book on Politics which has not survived. He repeatedly mentions this work in K. Tadbir al-Mutawaḥḥid, see pp. 4, 29, 55. (p. 4 : وقد لخصته فى العلم المدنى)

(27) Cf. Ibn Bāj., al-Samā', Fol. 53b: "Natural bodies, as explained are moved by something else, and so they cannot stop moving. A natural body is composed of 'mover' and 'moved' by way of definition and not by way of composition so that 'this', for example, would be in one part and 'that' in another part ;" (اما الاجسام الطبيعية فقد تلخص القول فيها وبين ان حركتها من غيرها ولذلك لايمكنها ان تقف بوجه و ان الجسم الطبيعى مؤلف من المحرك والمتحرك على جهة تاليف الحد لا على جهة التركيب حتى يكون هذا فى جزء و ذلك فى جزء آخر) .

(28) Natural bodies have place by nature, vide Arist. Phys. iv. 1. 208 b8; viii. 3.253 b 35.

(29) Ibn Bāj. defines قوة as a capacity through which a thing is described to be so and so; cf. Fol. 189b : القوة تقال على الاستعداد الذى يكون به الشيئ كذا و كذا See Arist. Met. 12.1019a 15.

(30) For the phrase like انحاء ما see the Ar. Text, Damascus, p. 61, Fol. 146A. حيوانات ما : al-Samā', Fol. 15b : اجسام ما ; also Ibn Sinā ; al-Shifā, Fol. 182a; يتخيل الوانا ما مشمول العين Fol. 183 b22: - او ان يكون الذى سببها اتصالات مالا يشعر بها . . . .

(31) The mover is not the same as the moved, but it is not possible to distinguish them in the elements, since they are simple and their parts are alike to each other. It is clear that everything that is inanimate is not mover, but is moved and 'being acted upon'; it is a mover only by being connected with a mover; Ibn Bāj. al-Samā', Fol. 50a:
فان المحرک ضرورة یجب ان یباین المتحرک وهذا شئی لایمکن فی الاسطقسات لانها بسائط ومتشابهة الاجزاء فقد بان ان کل ما لیس بذی نفس فلیس محرکا بل هو متحرک منفعل وانما هو محرک باقتران المحرک به .
Aristotle says: "so we are left with a mover, and a moved, and a goal of motion", vide Phys. v. I. 224 b 6.

(32) The Ar. Text, Fol. 143B, Damascus, p. 48;infra, pp. 26, 27:
یحرک حینا ولا یحرک کالثقل فی الحجر فانه -

(33) For, they do not need anything else to move them, because they have their mover in themselves ; Ibn Bāj. al-Samā', Fol. 48a : والمتحرکة بذواتها بعضها من تلقایها وهوالذی لا یحتاج فی تحریکه الی اٰخر غیره کانواع الحیوان Fol. 50a :
والصنف الثالث المتحرک من تلقایه وهو یتحرک کالحیوان وهو متحرک عن غیره لکنه فیه.
Cf. Arist. Phys. vii. 2.243a 14; viii. 4.254 b 15.

(34) Two movements are to be found in animate bodies, natural and unnatural; Ibn Bāj. al-Samā', Fol. 50a : وایضا فالمتحرکات بذواتها منها ما یتحرک طبعا، و منها ما یتحرک خارجا عنْالطبع وقسرا فان حرکة الحجر الی فوق هی خارجة عنالطبع، وقسرا لانه قد قهر علی ما فی طبعه ضده
Cf. Arist. Phys. viii. 3.254 b 20.

(35) To the Arab lexicographers روح , spirit, and نفس , soul, are synonyms; but to the philosophers these terms are analogous. Sometimes they are used in the sense of innate heat which is the first psychical organ, and where there is heat there is soul. The physicians, الاطباء , therefore, say that there are three souls, ارواح: (i) natural soul, روح طبیعی ; (ii) sensitive soul, روح حساس and (iii) moving soul, روح محرک . By طبیعی they mean the nutritive, because طبیعة in their art (i.e. طب) is said of the nutritive soul — it is applied to the soul not in so far as it is a soul, but in so far as it is a moving

soul. Thus the terms نفس and روح are two in expression but one in substratum. Moreover, in Anatomy they locate innate heat in heart, which is the source of life. See Tadbīr al-Mutawaḥḥid, p. 18 :
والروح يقال فى لسان العرب على ما يقال عليه النفس، ويستعمله المتفلسفون
باشتراک فتارة يريدون به الحارالغريزى الذى هوالالة النفسانية الاولى،
فلذلک ، نجد الاطباء يقولون ان الارواح ثلثة روح طبيعى و روح حساس
و روح محرک ويعنون بالطبيعى الغذائى اذ يوقعون الطبيعة فى صناعتهم
على النفس الغاذية' و يستعمل على النفس لا من حيث هى نفس بل من
حيث نفس محركة' والنفس والروح اثنان بالقول و احد بالموضوع.
al-Sama‘, Fol. 41a : و اماالروح الغريزى ففيه المحرک الذى لا يتحرک
و هذا يحرک الحيوان' و بهذا يوجدالحيوان متحركا من تلقايه و اذا
al-Hayawan, Fol. 96a : ذهب هذا الروح عند موت الحيوان
فهناک النفس و الالة الاولى بقيت تلک (المتوسطات) غيرمتحركه و لا
محركه . على ما تلخص فى الرابعة هى الحرارة الغريزية فحيث ينبوع الحرارة الغريزية
فهناک النفس' و الا القلب على ما شوهد بالتشريح هو ينبوع الحرارة الغريزية
فالقلب هو مبدأ الحيوان' فاما ان النفس حيث الالة الاولى فان ذلک
قد تبين فى الثامنة من السماع .

Text, Fol. 145A, Damascus also the Ar. p. 54 :
وهذه الحراة هى الة النفس

Cf. Arist. De Motu. Animalium, 10 54. 703 **a** 10 ; De Anima ii. 4.416 b. 29 ; Parv. Nat. 14 (viii), 474 a 25 et sq.

(36) Cf. Ibn Bāj. al-Samā‘, Fol. 8a : و ذلک ان من الاجسام ما يفعل
فعله دون الات كسموالنار و هبوط الحجر و صور امثال هذه تخص باسم
الطبيعة' و منها ما يفعله فعله بالات كاغتذاء النبات و حركة الحيوان'
و صور امثال هذه الاجسام يقال لها نفس .

(37) The first entelechy, in short, is the state when a body is prepared to receive anything without suffering change essentially not accidentally; see the Ar. Text, Fol. 155B. Damascus, p. 101, also the next note.

(38) The difference between the first and the last entelechy has been further explained by Ibn Bājjah. He says that a 'sleeping geometer' or one who is not geometrising is a potential geometer, but not like the beginner who has just started learning geometry. For the potency of the beginner is 'ignorance' جهل, or the like, whereas the

'sleeping geometer' possesses a state contrary to جهل and so he cannot be called جاهل, ignorant, as the term جاهل applies to the one who does not know geometry. He further says that when soul is said of the first entelechy it is a passive faculty, and when of the last an active faculty. But the plant has been given the last entelechy only ; and the first entelechy has not been given to it separately, and hence, it does not possess sense-perception which is the first entelechy, its last entelechy being things that have no limit and are essentially unlimited, and limited only accidentally. See al-Samā', Fol. 49a and b : و كذلك المهندس عند ما ينام او عند ما لا يستعمل علمه بالهندسة فهو مهندس بالقوة على غير هذا الوجه الذى به المتعلم مهندس، فان قوة المتعلم هى اما جهل او يقترن بها جهل، و اما النايم اوالذاهل عن علمه فليس قوته جهلا و لا مقترنة بجهل بل هو على حال مقابلة للجهل فان المهندس النايم ليس يصدق ؛ عليه جاهل بالهندسة كما يصدق على من لا يعلمها من الناس الطبيعيين also the Ar. Text, Fol. 155A, Damascus, p. 10
و اعنى بقولى الاول كما يقال فى المهندس حينما لا يستعمل عمله بالهندسة، و الموسيقار حين ما لا يستعمل صناعة الموسيقى يستعمل الاحن: Fol. 220 b فالنفس اذا قيلت على الكمال الاول كانت . قوة منفعلة و اذا قيلت على الكمال الاخير كانت قوة فاعلة، الا ان النبات اعطى كماله الاخير ولم يعط الكمال الاول مفراد ولذلك لم يوجد للنبات حس، فان الحس كمال اول وكماله الاخير امور غير محدودة بل هى بذات غير متناهية و انما تتناهى بالعرض - See the Ar. Text, Fol. 155A, Damascus, p. 101

(39) ان النفس هى الاستكمال الاول -
Cf. Arist. De An. iil. 402b 5

(40) In Logic, when a noun has a meaning that applies to some of the individuals more forcibly and in preference to other the noun is called مشكك, and the state تشكيك. The word تشكيك means "to doubt" and is used in equivocal and ambiguous sense. Vide M. 'Ali al-Thānawī, Kashshāf Iṣṭ ilāḥāt al-Funūn ed. Sprenger, p. 780 ; also Goichon : Lexique, p. 162.

(41) Cf. Arist. De An. i. I. 402A.

(42) Cf. Arist. De An. i. 1. 402 a 4.

(43) Ibn Sīna in his commentary on Aristotle's De Anima writes : اما معونتها في العلم الطبيعي فظاهر، لانها تعرف احوال الحرث والنسل، ولان السماء ايضا تتحرك بالنفس . . . . . و اما في العلم الالاهي فلان من النفس يتوصل الى معرفة الامور المفارقة، و تصور كيفية الادراك بالعقل -
See Badawī, A. R. : Arisṭū 'Ind al-Arab, p. 75.

(44) Cf. Ibn Bāj., Fol. 209a and b : والعلوم اليقينية ثلثة : احدها اليقين بوجود الشيء فقط و هو علم الوجود، و قوم يسمونه علم ان الشيء، والثاني اليقين بسبب وجود الشيء فقط، و قوم يسمونه علم لم الشيء، والثالث اليقين بهما جميعا -
Cf. Arist. Met. iii. 2. 996 b14 ; 1030 b20 ; 1086 b5 ; 1086b33 ; 999b26 ; Anal. Pos. i. 11 ; 19.100 a ; 6 i. 24. 85b13 ; see also Zeller : Aristotle, vol. i. p. 194.

(45) Cf. the Ar. Text, infra, Fol. 140B, Damascus, p. 33
و ايضا فان من العلوم . . . اولا علم ما الشيء -

(46) Cf. Arist., An. Pos. iii. 10.93B, 29.
Ibn Rushd defines حد as an expression that defines the nature of a thing through its essential characteristics which constitute the thing ; see Talkhiṣ Ma Ba'd al-Ṭabī-'ah, Hayder p.44.

(47) Cf. Arist. Phys. ii. 3.194 b 23.

(48) The scribe has repeatedly written this word as اللفت which is obviously wrong ; see Fol. 95a : فلذلک اللفت (الفت) من امثال هذه -

(49) Cf. Ibn Bāj. Fol. 211b and 212a : و كل واحد من هذه (اى الاسباب) اما قريب و اما بعيد. . . فان السبب الذى بالذات لا بد ان يكون قريبا او بعيدا او اعم او اخص او بالقوة او بالفعل. -

(50) Cf. Ibn Baj. al-Samā', Fol. 5b : و وجد العلم بوجودها اولا في الثلاثة التى هى المادة والصورة والفاعل بيناء و وجد الرابع هو الغاية مشكوكا فيه -
Fol. 211a: فقال و الاسباب اربعة فعددها -
Cf. Arist. Phys. ii. 3.195 a 15 ; 194 b23-195b21 ; Met. Δ 2 ; An : Pos. 94 a 20.

(51) Cf. Arist. An. Pos. ii. 13. 97 b 25—30.

(52) Ibn Bājjah often refers to the methods of induction : vide al-Ḥayawān, Fol. 92a : فاسباب الشئ قديدرک بالحس و قديدرک بالقول و ذلک اما بالنقسم او بالتركيب او بالبرهان او بالدليل .
فان الحدود كما قيل فى انا لوطيقى al-Athār al-'Ulwīyah, Fol. 71b : تولف اما بطريق التقسيم او بطريق التحديد او بطريق البرهان وهذا الطريق غير طريق كتبها بقراطيس. - Cf. Arist. An. Pos. ii. 5.91 b 12 ; Phys. viii. 1.252a 24, also Ibn Rushd : al-Sama', Hyderabad, p. 21.

(53) Cf. Arist., An. Pos. i.-2.72 a 15—24 ; ii. 9.93 b 21.

(54) Cf. Arist. An. Pos. ii. 10 94 a 21.

(55) Cf. Arist. An. Pos. ii. 10.94 a 2, a 21.

(56) Aristotle defines ' sign ' as a demonstrative proposition necessary or generally approved ; cf. An. Pos. ii. 27.70a 7.

(57) Cf. Arist. De An. i. 1. 402 a 12.

(58) Ibid. a 22 sq.

(59) Democritus held that " soul " is a substance consisting of indivisible and inseparable parts ; vide Ibn Bāj. al-Kawn, Fol. 80b : او اجزاء لا تنقسم و لا تنفصل كما يراها ديمقراطيس. Cf. Arist. De An. i.2.404 a 1.; 405 a 10.

(60) Cf. P. Kraus and Walzer : Galeni Compendium Timaei Platonis, text, p. 6 : وجعل النفس التى فيه من الجوهر الذى لا ينقسم الباقى دائما بحال واحدة و من الذى ينقسم فى الاجسام p. 7 ; ثم ان طيماؤس من بعد هذا الكلام يصف كيف تنقسم نفس العالم فى جميع اجزائه: p. 9 ثم قال فلما اتم خلق العالم قسم الانفس و جعل عددها كعددا لكواكب وصير كل واحد منها ; فى واحد من الكواكب واراها طبيعة العالم و سن لها السنن و بينها لها - ; also Bergstrasser : Galeni in Hippocratis De Septimanis, اعنى النفس فجزاها باجزاء سبعة' فقال ان النفس سبعة اجزاء' فاعلموانه ليس ابقراط وحده قال ان النفس مركبة من اخزشتى p. 100 سبعته لكن ذكر اكثر افاضل الفلاسفة و وجوههم شبه افلاطون و اصحابه -

(61) Plato believes that soul is separable—separable in form which implies that souls have actually no finiteness. See Ibn Bāj.
Fol. 187b : و لذلک لما رأى فلاطن ان النفس مفارقة' مفارقة معنى' ولزم عن هذا ان تكون انفس بلانهاية بالفعل.

Cf. Plato : Timaeus, trans. Jowett, vol. iii. 35,37 ; Arist. De Ani. i. 2.404 b 16.

(62) Cf. Arist. De An. i. 1.403 a 10.
also Ibn Rushd, Talkhiṣ K. al-Nafs, ed, Ahwani, p. 11.

(63) Ibn Bājjah often uses the phrase ازسع على and, ازسع ان vide al-Ḥayawān, Fol. 91b : ان كان هذاالعلم سنسعا ان يكون ; Fol. 91a : ان كان سن سعا ان يجرى Tadbir, ed. Asin Palacios, p. 61 ; see also note No. 10.

(64) Cf. Arist. De An. i. 1. 403 a 5—15 sq. : 403 a 28 ; 403 b 16 ; 402 a 6.

(65) Cf. Arist. An. Pos. 97 b 7 ; ' 28.

(66) Ibn Bājjah compares جنس , genus, with ماده , matter, and فصل , differentia, with صورة , form, since Aristotle describes matter, ماده , as potentiality and form, صورة , as actuality ; vide De An. ii. 1.412 a 10. The source of this comparison can be traced in Aristotle's Metaphsics, 1043 a 19 : " For the formula that gives the differentiae seems to be an account of the form and the actuality, while that which gives the components is rather an account of the matter".

(67) Cf. Arist. Met. z. 12. 1037 b 29 sq.
Ibn Rushd : Tafsir Ma Ba 'd al-Tabi'ah, ed, Bouyges, pp. 947 ; 951 ; 956.

(68) See note No. 52 *supra*.

(69) Cf. Arist. De An. i. 402 a 18—20.

(70) This word is frequently used by Ibn Bājjah; see Tadbir, p. 31; al-Samā', Fol. 9a: متى وجدت التام بها امر رابع ; Fol. 8b : ولا يليتم وجود بعض الاجسام لايليتم وجود الشئى الا به

(71) Cf. Arist. De An. i. I, 402 b 4.

(72) "This purpose" refers to the study of Political Science.

(73) As for the compound that has parts alike to each other and to the whole, it is like gold and bronze; cf. Ibn Bāj. al-Ḥayawan, Fol. 93b : واما مركبة متشابهة الاجزاء كالذهب والنحاس -

(74) This bears evidence that the book was available in Arabic inIbn Bājjah's time. But, I think, Ibn Bājjah means Al-Fārābi's

commentary on the paraphrase of Aristotle's De Anima by Alexander which has been mentioned by Al-Qifṭi as كتاب شرح الاسكندر فى النفس (vide Tarikh, Leipzig, p. 279 under al-Fārābi). So far as the philosophical texts are concerned, Ibn Bājjah mainly relies on the works of al-Fārābi, as is evident from what he says in the end of Risālat al-Wadā' Fol. 219b : وكر رالقول فيها ابو نصر وسكانه من هذالعلم سكانه ، لكن لا يوجد فى جميع كتبه التى وصلت الى الاندلس هذا النحو من النظر

(75) Cf. Arist. De An. ii. 2.414 a 16.

Ibn Sinā in his <u>Sh</u>ifā (Fol. 156a) precisely concludes this discussion and says: "Then, soul is a first entelechy, and since an entelechy is said of a thing, soul is the entelechy of a 'thing'. The 'thing' is the body . . . . And the body is not an entelechy for the soul which possesses it"; فالنفس كمال اول ، ولان الكمال كمال الشئى فالنفس كمال لشئى وهذا الشيئى هو الجسم وليس هذا الجسم لذى النفس كماله -

(76) Ibn Sinā explains that soul is not an entelechy of an artificial body, e.g. couch, and chair and the like; but it is an entelechy of a natural body, but not of every natural body, for soul is not an entelechy of earth nor of fire. Soul, in our world, is an entelechy of a natural body that produces its second entelechies through organs that help her in the activities of life, the first of which being nutrition and growth. Thus, we define soul as the first entelechy of an organized natural body which can perform the activities of life"; فانه ليست كمال الجسم الصناعى كالسرير والكرسى وغيره ، بل كمال الجسم الطبيعى ، ولا كل جسم طبيعى ، فليس النفس كمال ارض ولا نار ، بل هى فى عالمنا كمال جسم طبيعى يصدر عنه كمالاته الثانية بالات يستعين بها فى افعال الحيوة التى اولها التغذى والنمو ، فالنفس التى نحدها هى كمال اول لجسم طبيعى ; الى له ان يفعل افعال الحيوة -

see also notes 35 and 38.

(77) The phrase طبيعى الى organised natural, is not like the expression الكلب النباح the barking dog, because the latter expression is composed of synonyms, since نباح is not

only a differentia of الكلب here; Ibn Bājjah, al-Samā', Fol. 48b : فقولنا المتحرک الذی لیس واحد من هذین مرکب ترکیب ترادف وتعاون کقولنا الکاب النباح لا ان النباح فصل الکلب

(78) Cf. the Ar. Text, Fol. 140 B, Damascus, p. 33; also Ibn Rushd: T. al-Nafs, ed. Ahwani ; p. 12.

(79) Cf. Arist. De An. ii. 2.413 b II.

(80) "According to the author of the Ta'rīfāt, there are five kinds of substances at bottom of all realities : primal matter, form, body, soul and intelligence. Primal matter is the substance which is capable continuity or discontinuity and receives corporeal and specific forms. Corporeal form is that which is at once apprehended by the senses. Body is the substance which assumes the three dimensions, or extended substances. Soul or animal spirit is a subtle substance which supports the vital forces, capability of sensation, and liberty of movement; it is attached to the body. Intelligence or reasoning soul is a substance putrified of matter and linked up with the body which it governs", Enc. of Islam, vol. i, p. 1027, Djawhar.

Al-Fārābi defines the primary substances as (the specific) individuals which exist by themselves, and the secondary substances as the species and genera which exist through individuals ; see Masa'il Mutafarriqa, Hyderabad, pp. 7-8 ed. Dieteric, p. 89.

Ibn Sinā has devoted a chapter in his Shifā to the problem that soul comes under the category of substance. He says . "From what has been said it is clear that the soul is not body. Now if it is proved that no soul can essentially be constituted separately then there will remain no doubt that it is substance". He concludes his discussion by saying: "The soul is not an accident that does not make species diverse nor does play any part in the constitution of the substratum. Soul is, therefore, an entelechy like substance not like accident. This does not imply whether it is separable or not. For every substance is separable, since neither matter is separable not form."; see Bodl. MS. Proc. 125, Fol. 158b: فصل فى ان النفس داخلة فى مقولة" الجوهر . . . فالنفس اذن ليست من الاعراض التى لايختلف بها الانواع ولا يكون لها مدخل في تقويم الموضوع، فالنفس اذن كمال كالجوهر لا كالعرض، وليس يلزم هذا ان يكون مفارقا او غير مفارق فانه ليس كل جوهر بمفارق فلا الهيولى مفارقة ولا الصورة -

In the library of the Royal Asiatic Society of Bengal, Calcutta, there is a small MS. entitled رسالة للارسطا طاليس فى النفس which contains eight small chapters, the third chapter being on the problem that "the soul is substance". Here is the full chapter : الفصل الثالث، كل قابل للمتضادات وهو بالعدد واحد فهو جوهر، والنفس قابلة للبر والفجور والجراءة والجبن متضادات، فالنفس جوهر، وايضا فان كل متحرک للجوهر من ذاته هو جوهر، والنفس محركة للجسم الذى هو جوهر فالنفس اذا جوهر، وايضا فان النفس جزء من الجوهر الذى هوالحيوان لان كل حيوان نفس و جسم و جزء كل جوهر جوهر فالنفس اذن جوهر -

(81) See supra note 58.

(82) Cf. Arist. De An. i, 2.405 a 22; '25; 405 b 1 sq.

(83) Probably Ibn Bāj. refers to the views of Anaxagoras (cf. De An. i, 2.405 a 14), Empedocles (De An. 404 b 11) and others.

(84) Cf. Al-Farabi : Masā'il Mutafarriqa, Hyd. p. 19; Dieterici, p. 99.

(85) Cf. Arist. De An. i, 2.403 b 25.

(86) Cf. Ibn Bāj. Fol. 33b : فان كان محرک ما اول يحرک لابان يتحرک عن غيره فذلک متحرک بذاته فالى هنا انتهى النظر بافلاطون ولذلک رسم النفس انها شئى يحرک ذاته غير ان القول لم يلزم ان مثل هذا لا يحركه غيره بالاطلاق، بل انما لزم عنه انه لا يحركه محرک خارج عنه فانما الزم محال ما -

Cf. Arist. Phys. viii, 9.265 b 33; De An. i, 2.404 a 20; 406 b 11; '27.

(87) Ibn Bājjah explains in al-Samā' (Fol. 33b quoted above, see note 86) that although Plato holds that soul is self-mover it does not necessitate that such self-mover cannot be moved by something else absolutely, but it implies that it is not to be moved by a mover from outside which

leads to an absurdity. For everything that stops moving by the stopping of something else is evidently moved by something else. Hence, Aristotle concludes that everything moved has a mover other than itself absolutely; see also Fol. 35b : وارسطو سما نظر فى هذه الامور و وجد قولنا كل ما يكف عن الحركة . . . فمحركه غيره بالاطلاق -

(88) Cf. Ibn Bāj. Fol. 53b; Arist. Phys. vii, 2.243 a 13; vii. i, 241b 24. sq.; viii, 5.256 a 13.

(89) Cf. Arist. De An. i, 3.406 a 1.

(90) Here, by النفس Ibn Bāj. obviously means the faculties of soul.

(91) The phrase قد يظن clearly indicates that Ibn Bājjah does not favour this view, and he is one with Aristotle who thinks, that insects possess sensation and local movement, and also imagination and appetition; vide Arist. De An. ii, 2.413 b 20-32; 414 a1; '29; also Ibn Rushd, Talkhīṣ K. al-Nafs ed. Ahwāni, p. 174.

(92) Cf. Arist. Ibn Rushd: T., al-Nafs, ed. Ahwānī, p. 13.

(93) Cf. Arist. De An. ii, 4.415 a 23.

CHAPTER II

DISCOURSE ON THE NUTRITIVE FACULTY

This chapter starts with the description of " the being " in which the nutritive faculty is to be found.

" Being " is opposed to " not-being ", not-being can either not exist at all or it is possible that it comes to be. By ' possible ' is meant either that whose non-existence is impossible or that which can exist at any time. Since the substratum of the possible and that of the potential is one and the same, the terms " possibility " and " potentiality " mean the same. The potential, however, precedes the actual which is divisible into ten categories, and becomes actual only due to a change that occurs in essence, quality, quantity, and space—the four faculties that move the object and are called Passive Faculties.

The thing moved is either moved eternally or not eternally. The mover of the eternal movement is always one actual being but the mover of the transitory movement may be one or more than one, moving at a certain time and not moving at certain other times. The moving faculties are, again, of two kinds , those that exist in bodies, as e.g. forms or accidents and those that do not exist in bodies, as e.g. the Active and the Acquired Intellects. The souls of the spherical bodies are however, no faculties, and are called moving faculties only in so far as they are indentified with the Active Intellect.

Now, the moving faculty that acts in the food and transforms it into actual nutriment (i.e. blood or flesh) lies in the nutrient body. Since the nutritive soul is an agent that exists actually, it has two perfections : its existence as a faculty, and its existence as a moving agent.

Again, since every transitory being has to perform a particular function in virtue of which it stands as a part of the universe, the nutritive faculty has two ends, namely, the faculty of growth and the faculty of reproduction. This faculty does not only provide substances which are needed for the upkeep of a body, but also a surplus which is employed for the growth and development of the body. But when the growth is completed the surplus is used for reproduction in those bodies that are reproductive.

The faculty of reproduction is to be distinguished from the nutritive faculty which acts in the food and makes it a part of the body ; this faculty is the "actual intellect" that renders a potential species a body of the same species.

Those bodies that are not reproductive have existence alone and depend, for the preservation of their species, upon things of generation, e.g. spontaneous generation through putrefying heat.

The reproductive faculty is the end of the faculty of growth and perishes only in old age when the nutritive faculty is left alone.

(1) Cf. Ibn Bāj. al-Samā', Fol. 55a: الموجود يقابله لا موجود، وبينهما ما هو موجود ولا موجود لكن لا فى وقت واحد، وهذه كلها اما .الاطلاق او عند شئى ما فما هو لا موجود اصلا وهو الممتنع والمحال فبين امره -

(2) Ibn Bājjah uses the terms ضرورى ، ممكن الوجود and ممتنع الوجود as follows: (al-Samā Fol. 43 b,) و كل معنى معقول فهو ضرورة انما ممتنع وجوده او ضرورى وجوده او ممكن -

(3) Otherwise, it is absurd to assume something possible and assign to it an unlimited time which entails the existence of unlimited things; vide al-Samā', Fol. 46a: فكل ماانزلناه ممكنا وزمانا غير متناه لزم من ذلک وجود اشيا غير متناهية معاً، فان الممكن و الوجود فى زمان غير متناه محال -

(4) The term عدم, non-existence or privation, is defined as "that which does not exist so and so, i.e. privation of so and so", for absolute non-existence has no existence. The term non-existence is always relative, because "privation" means "privation of something"; Ibn Rushd : Tafsīr Ma-Ba'd al-Ṭabi'ah, ed. Bouyges, ii, p. 801; also see next note.

(5) Ibn Bajjah explains, in al-Samā' Fol. 7a, that ممكن, possible, is followed by عدم, privation, by necessity. He then asks whether 'possibility' is 'privation', like 'form' which is 'being', or not, and then answers: "We say, the possible in so far as it is possible has essentially no privation, because 'possibility' is the second substratum for the 'form' at the time when this substratum suffers

privation. Privation is essentially nothing, nor does anything at all proceed from it, its essence and quiddity being 'not-being'. Possibility, on the other hand, exists in the being of a thing. But privation happens to the possible not in so far as it is possible, but it has possibility in one respect and privation in an other respect. Privation only causes alteration in the possible"; . . , والممكن لزمه العدم ضرورة فهل الامكان هو العدم كما الصورة هي الوجود ام لا' فنقول: ان الممكن من طريق ما هو ممكن فليس للوجود لذاته عدم' فان الامكان هو ثاني الموضوع للمعنى عند ما عرض لذلك الموضوع العدم، فان العدم ليس هو بالذات، لايوجد عنه الشئ اصلا' بل ذاته وماهيته الاتوجد' والامكان و ما هو فوجوده في ان يوجد الشئ' فالعدم عارض للممكن لا من جهة ما هو ممكن بل الامكان فيه من جهة والعدم من جهة ما، الممكن شئ اخر كانك قلت نحاس اوصورة مضادة فلذلك يكون وجود المعنى في الممكن تماما لا استحالة، وانما يكون استحالة" الممكن من جهة العدم).

Cf. Arist. Phys. i, 3.187 a 4 sq.

(6) That potentiality precedes actuality in time has been repeatedly referred to by Ibn Bājjah; Fol. 44b: "فاذا القوة متقدمة للكمال بالزمان Fol. 52a: من تقدم القوة للفعل بالزمان ; Fol. 93b : ان قوة كل موجود سابقة لفعله بالزمان

Cf. Arist. Met. B. 6.1003 a 1.

But this seems to be contrary to what Aristotle holds that the actual is prior to the potential in time; vide Met. 0. 8. 1049 b 18.

(7) Cf. Ibn Baj. al-Sama', Fol. 10b: والشئ اذا كان بالقوة جملة فليس هو بالفعل شيئا مما هو بالقوة ذلك الشئ، واذا كان بالفعل جملة فليس هو بالقوة اصلا ذلك الشئ ولا فيه جزء من اجزاء القوة.

(8) Cf. the Ar. Text Fol. 150a, Damascus, p. 80. كل ما بالقوة فانما يصير بالفعل الخ' al-Samā', Fol. 35a; فان الفعل لا يتحرك وانما يتحرك ما بالقوة . . . . فالمغالبة ضرورة في التغير يحتاج الى ثلثة اشياء ـ متقابلان و موضوع ـ والموضوع هو ما بالقوة وهو قابل للتغير

Cf. Arist. Phys. viii, 4.255 a 34-35 5.257 b 7;

Ibn Sīnā, Shifā, Fol. 196 b 8;

وكل ما خرج من القوة الى الفعل فانما يخرج بسبب بالفعل يخرجه.

(9) Cf. Ar. Text Fol 144 a, Damascus, p. 51. والتغير كما قلنا ; يكون في الجوهر : 32b و ذلك هو التغير في الجوهر ; al-Samā', Fol. 16a لما كان المتغير منه ما يقال بالتقديم ومنه ما يقال بالتاخير، فالمقول بالتقديم هو ما في الجوهر و في الكم وفي الكيف والاين على ما تلخص في الثالثة.;

Ibn Bājjah explains the cause of the change that occurs in the four categories as follows: "The investigation here is about the first cause which in so far as it is existence is called change. But the first cause in so far as it is form is not one, nor has a single expression. Now the categories whose definitions are axiomatic are four: (a) substance, its first being 'generation', (b) quantity having growth as its first being, and diminution being suitable to not-being — these have contraries, generation opposing corruption, and growth diminishing—(c) quality, its contrary being called 'alteration' whose neither extreme is fitter to be called 'being' than the other; and (d) movement in space, i.e. locomotion which is the fittest for existence, since it contains nothing that can eliminate the existence of the being; cf. al-Samā', Fol. 10a: لكن الفحص عنه هنا فمن جهة الوجود الذى يقال له تغير ' واماالسبب الاول الذى على طريق الصورة فليس بواحد ولا يوجد له قول واحد فانما يعطى بحدودها وهى المقولات الاربع وهو الجوهر والوجود الاول فيه كون ' والكم والوجود الاول فيه نمو ' واما النقص فاحرى ان يكون "لاوجود" وهذه تقابلها اضداد، فالكون يقابله الفساد والنمو يقابله الذبول ، والكيف و يقال لصندته استحالة وليس احد طرفيها اخلق بان يكون وجودا من الاخر فليرسما فيالوجود، والحركة فيالاين وهى النقلة وهذه اخلق بالوجود من سايرها' اذ ليس فيها سايزيل بالذات وجود الموجود -

(10) Cf. Ibn Bāj. al-Samā', Fol. 29b: "وتغيرت النسب و تبدلت نسبة بعد نسبة اخرى لكن هذه و ان لم تكن تغيرا فهى عن تغير لكن ذلك التغير فى شئى اخر و يكون للنسب تغير تابع لتغير فلذلك يكون فى الان -
Ar. Text Fol. 153a; Damascus, p. 92. ويكون تغيرها فى الان ; Zeller: Aristotle, vol. i, p. 433, 9.

(11) For Relation requires two substrata mover and moved, which must be different from each other; vide Ibn Bāj. Fol. 61a:
فان المحرك والمتحرك من المضاف فيجب ضرورة ان يكون فى موضوعين تغاير ما حتى يكونا اثنين -

(12) The infinitive is مساوقة, to accompany, see Dozy: Lexique, i. p. 704; Cf Ibn Bāj. al-Samā ', Fol. 26a : فحركة ح د تساوق اجزاوها - اجزاء اب و تتناسب تناسبها . . . و الزمان يساوقالطول بتوسط الحركة عليه

Zeller : Aristotle, i.p. 302 foot. note ;
Arist. De Gen. et Cor. i. 7. 324 a 9.

(13) Cf. Text. supra, Fol. 143a, Damascus p. 45 والممكن و ما بالقوة واحد بالموضوع

(14) Cf. Ibn Bāj. al-Kawn, Fol. 83a ; ليس يلزم ضرورة ان يكون كل قوة محركة فقوامها بجسم كما يلزم ان كل قوة متحركة فهى فى جسم و ذلک قد تبين فى السادسة من السماع .

(15) This is because motion cannot act upon that which is not divisible ; cf. Ibn Baj. Fol. 25a : فظاهر انه لا يكون حركة على ما لا ينقسم : al-Ḥayawan Fol. 96b : لكن كل متحرک فهو منقسم

(16) Cf. Ibn Rushd : Tafsīr, ed. Bouyges, p. 1637.

(17) Since our being in the sense that we understand is like our being in the sense that we see and touch—seeing and touching being no alteration—our being in the sense that we understand is no alteration. . .Man can use his intellect even he is deprived of movement, and when, for example, some of them are in deep meditation their senses stop functioning and they become as if they were asleep. In this state intelligence is apparent. As shown somewhere else, intelligence is not in time and so it has no motion. It is time which needs its existence ; vide Ibn Bāj. al-Samā', Fol. 38a : فان وجودنا ان نعقل كوجودنا ان نبصرونلمس و هذان ليسا استحالتين فلا وجودنا ان نعقل استحالة . . . فانما يعقل الانسان اذا سلبت جميع حركاته حتى ان بعضهم اذا استغرقوا فى الفكرة بطلت حواسهم و صاروا فى حال النيام و اذا كان ذلک، فعند ذلک يوجد العقل، و قد تبين فى غير هذا المكان ان العقل يوجد لا فى زمان فليس فيه حركة وانما يحتاج الزمان الى وجوده .

(18) Ibn Bājjah classifies " spiritual forms " (الصور الروحانية) in four kinds : (1) Forms of the spherical bodies, صور الاجسام المستديرة (2) Active and Acquired Intellect, العقل الفعال و العقل المستفاد, (3) the immattered intelligibles, المعقولات الهيو لانية, (4) the forms that are in the faculties of the soul, المعانى الموجودة فى قوى النفس, viz. those that are in the common sense, in the faculty of imagination and in the faculty of recollection ; vide Tadbir, p. 19.

(19) Self-moving things are composed of both mover and moved, and so the spherical body is sometimes regarded

to have been moved by nature, and sometimes by soul ; vide al-Samā : Fol. 54b :

فالمتحرک من تلقایه لما هو متحرک من تلقایه مولف من هذین و لذلک یقال فی الجسم المستدیر تا رة ان حرکة عن النفس

Fol. 121 a : ولکل جرم سمائی عقل و نفس

Fol. 95 b : فلذلک لزم ضرورة علی ما تلخص فی غیر هذا الموضع ان یکون محرک المستدیر عقلا ۔

Cf. Zeller : Aristotle, i. p. 477 ft. note.

(20) By 'last food' Ibn Baj. means 'the actual food. الغذاء بالفعل which is also called ' the near food ' and is that which is transformed into the substance of the nutrient. Before transformation food is called ' the potential food ' or 'the far food '. Cf. Ibn Rushd : Talkhis, ed. Ahwani, p. 15, Hyd. p. 12 ; also Text Fol. 144A, Damascus, p. 50.

(21) Ibn Bājjah seems to have been fond of symbols, he often tries to describe a word by its written form. For example , he describes the word روحانی by saying : وشکل هذه اللفظة غیر عربی و هی دخیلة فی لسان العرب ; cf. Tadbīr, p. 18.

(22) Cf. Ar. Text, Fol. 144 B, Damascus, p. 53.

(23) Cf. Arist. De An. ii. 4.416 a 11.

(24) Ibn Bājjah denies quantity growth. The piling of parts upon one another is no growth, and so quantity has no soul. Cf. Arist. De An.ii.4.416 a, 23—25.

(25) The plant takes nutriment and possesses nutritive soul. Hence they doubt whether the things between plant and stone possess soul or not. Similarly, they doubt whether things like the sponge of the sea, which come in between plant and animal and take share from both, possess nutritive soul or not ; see Ibn Bāj., al-Nabāt, Fol. 113b :

ان النبات هو مغتذ و له نفس غاذیة و لذلک یشک فی اشیاء توجد وسطا بین النبات و بین الحجر و کذلک یوجد جسم بین النبات و الحیوان یاخذ من کل واحد بقسط کاسفنج البحر .

Cf. Arist. Hist. Ani. I. 487 b 9 ; viii, 1. 588 b 20.

(26) See Ibn Bāj. : K. al-Nabāt, ed. Asin Palacios. al-Andalus, 1940, where Ibn Bajjah also maintains that man should be assumed as a genus different from animals—ape being the medium between them : (fol. 113 b : والوسط بین الاجسام

الطبيعة والاجسام المتنفسة هوالمتوسط بينهما و بين النبات، فانه لا وسط بين الاجسام المعدنية و بين الحيوان، لان الوسط انما هوابدا فيما بين الابعد و الاقرب و لذلک يوجد بين المتنفس المدرک و هوالحيوان غيرالناطق والمتنفس الذى لايدرک و هوالنبات وسط و من هنا فقد يجب ان نظن ان الانسان جنس آخر غيرالحيوان لان بينه و بين الحيوان غيرالمدرک وسطا و هو القرد

(27) Cf. Ibn Rushd : Talkhīṣ Ma Ba'd al-Ṭabī'ah, Hyderabad. p. 71. see also note, ii. 9.

(28) Cf. Ibn Bāj. Fol. 101a : و قد تبين ان الغذاء القريب هوالدم و تبين بيانا اتم فى اقاويل تكون الجنين : Fol. 113b ان كل نبات فهو مغتذ و كل مغتذ فهو على ما كتبناه فى كتاب النفس يستعمل حرارة طبيعة و بها تغير الغذاء، و غذاء النبات نبين بنفسه،

Arist. De. Gen. An. i.20.728 a 20 ; 726 b 1.

(29) Namely, the moving faculty which acts upon the substance (i.e. food).

(30) Cf. Ibn Bāj. Fol. 92a : و لما كان كالكمال صنفين : الحركة و الفعل، و الحركة التى هى التكون هى الكمال الاول .

Fol. 9a : و متى وجد الشئ كان على كماله الاخير و متى لم يوجد كان ناقصا

(31) In al-Kawn, Fol. 86 a, Ibn Bāj. explains that generation takes place at the time of alteration ; and generation is either simple or compound. By simple generation, he means, the change into a simple being, and by compound generation the movement towards a composite being ; فاما ان يكون التكون عند الاستحالة فذلک بين ; ibid . Fol. 81a : ان كل تكون فهواما بسيط و اما مركب اعنى بالتكون البسيط التغير الى الموجودالبسيط واعنى بالتكون المركب الحركة الى المجودالمركب).

Now Ibn Baj. asks : " which kind of generation is the generation of the nutritive soul ?".

(32) Cf. Ar. Text. Fol. 143 B, Damascus, p. 49: والغذاء يقال بالقوة الخ

(33) Ibn Rushd says : " The mover of the far nutriment is necessarily something other than the nutritive soul "; vide Talkhiṣ, ed. Ahwani, p. 15, Hyd. p. 12.

(34) Cf. Ibn Bāj. Fol. 101a : الغذاءالقريب هوالدم

(35) As stated by Aristotle, there are two sets of thinkers, one asserting that like is fed as well as increased in amount

by like, the other maintaining quite the opposite, viz. that what feeds and what is fed are contrary to each other (De Anima, ii. 4.416 a 30). " In solving this problem ", Aristotle further says, "it makes all the difference whether we mean by food the ' finished ' or the ' raw ' product. If we use the word food of both, viz. of the completely undigested and the completely digested matter we can justify both the rival accounts of it, taking food in the sense of undigested matter, it is the contrary of what is fed by it, taking it as digested it is like what is fed by it. Consequently it is clear that in a certain sense we may say that both parties are right, both wrong. "

The Arabic translation of the De Anima ascribed to Isḥāq Ibn Ḥunayn and published by al-Ahwāni, which is evidently not a translation but a commentary, probably written before Isḥāq Ibn Ḥunayn, throws light in this concern as follows : " Both these theories are right with regard to different kinds of food. This is so because ' food ' is of two kinds : actual and potential. The actual food is that which is changed, transformed into, and has become like the nutrient ; the potential is that which is not so "; see Ahwāni's edition of Talkhīṣ K. al-Nafs li 'Ibn Rushd, pp. 143-144. a Persian translation of this work is available in the Bodl Ous. 95, Fol. 41B—52B. This MS. discusses food as follows : Fol. 45a 17 : پس چنین گفت دانایٔ یونان که غذا دوگونه است ازان بود که بفعل غذا باشد و بود که بقوت غذا باشد اما غذایٔ بفعل بعد از استحالت بود که مانند تن غذا کننده بود، اما غذا بقوت آنکه هنوز گردیده حال نباشد و طعام که ناپخته بود هنوز غذا است و بتن غذا کننده نماند، و همچنین دیگر خورشها که بیرون تن باشد و نارسیده بتن هنوز و از حال نگردیده و مانند تن نشده آنرا بغذا نکنند الا دو نفس و ازین گفته شد که آتش غذا کننده نیست از انکه دو نفس نیست، و همچنین دیگر چیزها که نفس ندارند غذا نکنند -.

Ibn Bājjah however, categorically denies of any inconsistency between the two theories and says that the theory that ' food ' is from the opposite is true of the potential food, the other theory that it is from the like is true of the actual food. Cf. Arist. De Gen. er Cor.1.5.322a, 5 sq. ; Ibn Rushd ; Talkhīṣ, ed. Ahwani, p. 159.

(36) Cf. Ibn Rushd : Talkhīṣ, Maba'd al-Tabi'ah, Hyd. p. 55.

(37) Cf. Ar. Text supra, Fol. 143 B, Damascus, p. 48.

(38) Cf. Arist. De An. ii.4.416 b 14—15.

(39) This sentence explains the sentence on p. 33 : و كل قوة محركة ففيها مع انها موجودة الوجودالذى يخصها Ibn Bājjah perhaps means to say that the moving faculty is the same as generative faculty which acts in the food and makes out of food another body like its own body. Now this body reproduced by the faculty plays the part of a 'form' for the faculty, and moves it to continue its existence.

Cf. Arist. De An. ii. 416 b 24 ; 'b11-14.

(40) Cf. Ibn Bāj. Fol. 96a : فالعضوالذى فيه القوة الغاذية فهناك سايرالقوى و به تكون حياةالحيوان و هذا هو فى الانسان القلب و كذلك فى كل حيوان ذى دم و فى كل حيوان قلب او مايناسب القلب فى الحيوان الذى له مايناسب الدم ـ

also Fol. 96b ; فالنفس ضرورة فى الحيوان فى القلب او فيمايناسبه فالقلب مبداء الحيوان سايرالاعضاء واما حافظ له او متحرك عنه فكل ما فى الجسد هو تابع للقلب او ما يناسبه ـ

(41) Probably Ibn Bāj. refers to Fol. 96b, see the previous note.

(42) Ibn Bāj. obviously refers to what he has said in the beginning of this book, p.2 : فمتى كان الموجود. . .ان يختلط به غير واحد ;

Cf. Arist. De Gen.et Cor. ii.8.334 b 31 sq.

(43) Cf. Ibn Bāj. Fol. 81b : و كذلك الاسطقسات يماس كل واحد منها فى مواضعها الطبيعية...و قد تدنو هذه بعضها من بعض على احوال مختلفة ـ

Arist. De Gen. et Cor.i. cc. 6-10.

(44) In K. al-Ḥayawān, Fol. 109b, Ibn Bāj. explains that when two elements meet each other they do not get mixed together, but require a third power to move them and make them a single thing. This is not possible by the moving faculty which is called cold which can only freeze them and make them two limited things. It is

'heat' which mixes them first and then distributes them among the homogeneous limbs ; (فان الاسطقسين متى تقارنت قواهما لم يختلطا بل كان كل واحد منها يقدر على التخلص من صاحبه فلذلك يحتاج الى مبدأ آخر يؤلف بينهما و يحركهما حتى يصيرا شيئا واحدا و تصير قوتهما قوة واحدة مركبة، و هذا لا يكون بالقوة المحركة التى هى برد فان البرد يجمدهما و يجعل لكل واحد منهما نهاية تخصه، فلا يختلطان، و اما الحرارة فمن شانها ان يخلط اولا ثم يفرق بين المجانسة ثانيا و ثالثا)

Cf. Arist. De An. ii. 4.416b 29 ;' a 9 ; also Ibn Sina : Shifa', Fol. 163 a 20 : ثم ان "اله" هذه القوة (الغاذية) الا و لية هى الحار الغريزى "فان الحار هو المستعد لتحريك المواد و يتبعها البرد لتسكينها عند الكمالات من الخلق مختومة عليها

Ibn Rushd : Talkhīṣ, ed. Ahwani. p. 18, Hyd. p. 15.

(45) Cf. Ibn Bāj. fol. 98b : و كل محرك ليس بمتحرك بذاته فانما يحرك جسما على احد وجهين اما و هو فيه - و يكون ذلك الجسم المتحرك الاول من تلقايه، او يحرك جسما ليس هو فيه، فيحركه بتحريكه الجسم الذى هو فيه آلة لتحريك غيره : Fol. 41a و اما الروح الغريزى ففيه المحرك الذى لا يتحرك، و هذا يحرك الحيوان و بهذا يوجد الحيوان متحركا من تلقايه

(46) Cf. Ibn Rushd : Tal., ed, Ahwāni, p. 16 Hyd. p. 14.

(47) Cf. Arist. De Gen. et Cor. i. 10.328 b 4.

(48) Arist. De An. ii. 4.416b 19-20 ; also Ibn Sīna, Shifa, Fol. 162 b 9 : فالقوة الغاذية تورد البدل اى بدل ما يتحلل و يشبه و يلصق، و انه و ان كان الغذاء اكثر منافعه انه يقوم بدل ما يتحلل فانه ليست الحاجة الى الغذاء لذلك فقط بل تحتاج اليه الطبيعة فى اول الامر للتربية و ان كان بعد ذلك انما يحتاج الى وضعه موضع التحلل فقط

(49) Cf. Ibn Sīnā, Shifā', Fol. 162 b : والنامية تفعل فى اول كون الحيوان فعلا ليس هو التغذية فقط، و ذلك لان غاية التغذية ما حددناه، و اما هذه القوة فانها توزع الغذاء على خلاف مقتضى القوة الغاذية و ذلك لان الذى للقوة الغاذية لذاتها ان يوتى كل عضو من الغذاء بقدر عظمه و صغره و تلصق به من الغذاء بمقداره الذى له على السواء . و اما القوة النامية فانها تسلب جانبا من البدن من الغذاء ما يحتاج اليه الزيادة فى جهة اخرى فيلصقه بتلك الجهة ليزيد تلك الجهة فوق زيادة جهة اخرى مستخدمة الغاذية فى جميع ذلك، و لو كان الامر الى الغاذية لسوت بينها او لفضلت الجهة التى لقصتها الناسية

(50) Cf. Arist. De Gen. et Cor. i. 5.322 a 16-33.

(51) Cf. Ibn Bāj. al-Kawn, Fol. 81a : ولما كان الاختلاط قد يظن به انه نمو الاختلاط ; يظن انه اضمحلال لزمه ان يفحص ايضا عن هذه الحركة و يميزها بما يخصها

Arist. De Gen. et Cor. i.c 10.

(52) Cf. Arist. De Gen. et Cor. i.5. 322 a 23,

(53) Cf. Arist. De Gen. et Cor. i. cc 17-20, especially i. 19.726bI-2 ;—De An. ii 4.415 a 29 ; De Gen. An. ii. I. 735 a 16-19 ; also Ibn Rushd : Talkhīṣ, ed, Ahwāni, p. 16. Hyd. p. 14 ;

Ibn Sina summarizes the functions of the faculties of nutrition, growth and generation as follows : (Shifa',F ol. 163 a)

و بالجملة فان القوة الغاذية مقصودة ليحفظ بها جوهر الشخص والقوة الناسية مقصودة ليتم بها جوهر الشخص والقوة المولدة مقصودة ليستبقى بها النوع -

(54) Referring to Aristotle Ibn Bājjah says (vide Fol. 98 b : قد تبين فيىوىن الحيوان ان القوة المصورة فى المنى قوة عقلية لان فيها النوع مجردا ، ولم يبين كيف ذلک ...... انه بين ان الذى فى المنى هو قوة نوع الشخص المولد فقط فكيف ليت شعرى تقلبه وايضا فما هذا النوع واى وجود وجوده فان النوع متى صار عقلا بالفعل وذلک عند وجوده فى القوة الناطقة لم يمكن ان نعقل فى موضوعاته لانه غير مقترن بالته that the faculty that gives the semen form is an " intellectual faculty ", قوة عقلية , which contains the species as separated (from matter). It is clear that what is in the semen is exclusively the power of the species of the generative individual. But it is not known how does the semen possess this power. Again, what is this species, and what is the nature of its being? For when the species, becomes an 'actual mind'—and this happens when the species is in the rational faculty—we cannot understand its substrata, since it is not connected with its organ. Ibn Bajjah also says that man is in a way in common with the heavenly bodies, since man resembles them in so far as the power he contains is an actual mind (vide Fol. 107 b : بل الامر على مايقوله ارسطو انه مشارک بوجه ماللاجرام السماوية فان يشبهها من جهة ان القوة التى فيه عقل بالفعل Moreover, he identifies the 'actual mind' with the immattered forms as abstracted from matter' (vide, Text, infra, p. 59). He is more precise in his letter which he wrote after Risālat al-Wadā'

ولذلک بقبی بزرها (النفس المولدة) وبالجملة فاعلها اعنی (fol. 220 b :
الحار النفسانی سواء کان فی بزر اوفی الهواء اوالماء مبثوثا النوع و فیه
سافیه نوع نفس النبات معقولا فی جوهر هذا الفاعل عقل الهی کما یقوله ارسطو
فی السادسة عشر من کتاب الحیوان ولذلک لایحتاج الی محرک اخر
where he says " hence the sperm and, in short, the agent of the generative soul—I mean, the psychical warmth, no matter whether it is in the semen or in air or in water, since the species is scattered in all thęse, and it contains the species of the vegetative soul—remain as an object of mind. The substance of this agent is a 'Divine Mind', as has been shown by Aristotle in the sixteenth book of the book of Animals (cf. Arist. De Gen. An. i.19.726 b 15-24). And so it does not need any other mover."

But Aristotle does not precisely say that the cause of generation is 'Divine Mind'. He simply says : " . . and what each of them is actually such is the semen potentially, either in virtue of its own mass or because it has a *certain power* in itself . . . . ".

Ibn Bājjah probably toes the line of Ibn Sina who says: " When our soul comes out from potentiality to actuality in a single intelligible it becomes the intelligible an actuality and so, the Active Intellect, as it is, or a part of it, becomes one with it (i.e. the soul) ; or an impression of the Active Intellect is represented in the soul. Now if the soul becomes one with the Active Intellect as it is, then it becomes an actual mind in all intelligibles." (see His تعليقات on the De Anima published by A.R. Badawi under the title ' Arisṭū 'Ind al-Arab', p. 92).

The source of Ibn Bājjah and also of Ibn Sīna is evidently in al-Fārābi who holds that the agent that brings the intelligibles from potentiality to actuality is an essence whose substance is actual mind and separable from matter (vide Arāu Ahl al-Madinat al-Faḍila, ed. Dieterici. p. 44.). Ibn Bāj. as a matter of fact refers to al-Farābi when he says in " al-Ittiṣal " (published along with Talkhīṣ K. al-Nafs li'ibn Rushd ed. Ahwani, p. 107),

' So the actual mind is the first mover in man absolutely. And it is clear that the actual mind is an active power ... The reasoning faculty is primarily said of the spherical form in so far as it receives intellect, and is said of 'actual mind'. It is this power which Abū Naṣr means when he doubts by saying : 'Does it exist in the child, but is changed by moisture ? or does it arise in the end?"

This theory of Ibn Bājjah is also supported by Ibn al-Imām who makes a remark on the margin of his copy of Ibn Bājjah's text : " The power which makes the form determined in the species is not a power in the body but is an actual mind and is separable. " See also Ibn Rushd : Talkhiṣ, ed, Ahwani, p. 7 'Hyd. p. 5 ; also K. al-Nafs, ed. Ahwani p. 168 ; its Persian trans. Bodl. MS. Ous. 95. Fol. 50b 15 : وازان گفتیم که آنچه بقوت دانده آن بود بفعل داننده شود که تابدانست بقوت داننده بودو چون بدانست بفعل داننده شد، واین فعل آنگه افتد که عقل در تن بود اما چون با خود رود جدا از تن بفعل باشد و در دانستن چیز ها حاجتمند حس نباشد

(55) Ibn Bājjah further differentiates between the functions of the nutritive and the generative faculties by saying that when the nutritive faculty acts in a suitable substance to generate its species the forms (i.e. the generative faculty) moves and causes this movement.

This is in conformity with Aristotle who says that just as nutrition preserves individuals, so does generation perpetuate the species ; vide, De An. ii. 415 a 29.

(56) Cf. Ibn Sīna, Shifā, Fol. 163a : فالغاذية تورد بدل ما يتحلل من الشخص، والمولدة تورد بدل ما يتحلل من النوع

(57) According to Ibn Bājjah, unlike art, for example, that gives form to the wood, the faculty of generation not only reproduces something like it but it is also connected with the body.

(58) Aristotle, though does not deny spontaneous generation, categorically refutes the view of the early philosophers who held that some living things arose out of putrefaction, since he says that " nothing comes into being by putrefying, but concocting ; putrefaction and the thing

putrefied is only a residue of that which is concocted (cf. De Gen An. iii. 11.762 a 14 and 15). " But the K. al-Nafs ascribed to Iṣhaq and its Persian translation describe this view in a way as if Aristotle held it (see ed. Ahwani, p. 173-'4) ; Fol. 52a 19 : وگفت ما همی بینم جانوران و همچنین: Fol. 49 a 5 ; ناقص راکه از بوسیدن رطوبات خیزدکه همی روند حس در هر جانوری بود ووهم نه همه را بود که از جانورانچه از عفونات ستولد شد چون انواع کرم و مگس بے حس نباشند و وهم نبود ایشانرا از آنکه ماوای ندارندکه باز شناسند از وافعالی که بوهم تعلق دارند ۔

Ibn Bājjah and Ibn Rushd, however, state categorically that some living beings, e.g. flies, bugs and the like, come into being from putrefaction ; cf. Fol. 98a :كالذباب والبراغيث وما جانسها ۔ وهى التى تتولد عن العفونة ۔

Ibn Rushd, Talkhīṣ, ed. Ahwani, p. 55.

Their statement is obviously based on what Aristotle says in Meteorology, iv, 1. 379 b 6, that animals are generated in putrefying bodies ; see also iv. 1.379 a 16 ; 389 b 5.

(59) Aristotle defines تالى , successive, as " that which is after the beginning (the order being determined by position or form or in some other way) and has nothing of the same class between it and that which it succeeds, (Met. 1068 b 30)".

(60) Ibn Bājjah. speaks of. اتصال الوجود later on, see Ar. Text p. 50. (infra)

(61) Cf. Ar.Text supra, Fol.148 A, Damascus p. 71, pp. 37-38.

(62) Cf. Ibn Bāj. Fol. 108 b: وهى التى هم موضوعة لتفعل منها البزرو هى الطمث ويسميه ارسطو بزرا .

Cf. Arist. De Gen. Am. i. 16. 721 b 5 sq.

(63) Ibn Rushd uses تمام instead of طرف , cf. Talkhīṣ, ed. Ahwani, p. 19.

(64) Ibid.

(65) Cf. Ibn Bājja, Fol. 220 b : بل النفس المنهية توجد فى اول العمر وتعدم بعد ذلک ، والنفس المولدة لا توجد فى اول عمر الجسم الحى ثم توجد بعد ذلک ولا تعدم الابعرض وقد شوهد شيوخ تنسلوا بعد الثمانين ۔

CHAPTER III

DISCOURSE ON THE FACULTIES OF SENSE-PERCEPTION.

In this chapter, Ibn Bājjah explains the mutual relation of 'form' and 'matter', and describes what happens to matter or form when one is separated from the other. Matter is always connected with form, but when it is separate and a mere substratum it is capable of receiving a form which, when it comes to it, sets it into motion. But although matter can potentially move and be separate from form, form cannot be separated from matter except by accident. Hence, when form is abstracted from matter it is not entirely separate and continues to have some sort of connection with matter—this connection has been designated as 'the connection in existence" since immattered forms are either perceivable or imaginable, when imaginable they are not material but are images of material beings.

There are different grades of form : (a) form existing in matter, (b) form as existing in the intellect but requiring a material substratum. But an immattered form cannot be separated from matter, since its relation with matter is due to matter itself, and hence, so long it is connected with matter it is intellect, and when matter is abstracted it becomes a potential intellect. Separation is of different grades—every grade being called soul, and a spherical faculty—as *e. g.* sense-perception, imagination and reasoning.

Sense-perception is either actual or potential. What is potential can only become actual when it is changed by something else. It, therefore, requires a mover to change it—this mover is the sensible, the moved being the sense organ.

The sensibles or the natural accidents are of two kinds : either they are particular to the natural bodies or common to the natural and the artificial bodies ; and they are, again, either mover or moved. They are always moved towards the species, since a mover causes motion in them only in so far as they are particular species, and not because they possess matter.

Every sentient body is composite and is the result of a mixture of different elements. This mixture is produced by the innate heat and gives rise, for example, to condensation and rarefaction, odour, flavour and colours. But besides these material states, there arise certain other states, such as reproduction and spontaneous generation, which are caused by "Intellect" or some other movers.

As soon as the process of mixture begins the form begins to be received. Motion and reception of form takes place simultaneously; and when the soul attains perfection the reception of form is completed—matter and form thus become a single whole. But when form is separated from matter it exists actually as abstract from matter, but is not the same as it is when it is in the matter—and this is possible only when it is in the mind.

Sensation is, therefore, transitory, but how can a separate form be transitory, since transitoriness is only due to matter? The answer is this. The term 'matter' is used for 'psychical faculty' and 'corporeal faculties' equivocally, and matter here means only the receptivity of form through which a body that has a faculty like this is said to become sentient.

The faculty of sense-perception is, therefore, a capacity in the sense organ that becomes a form of the thing perceived.

But a question arises: If perception is in a different matter then how can matter actually exist when it is not matter! The answer is given as follows. That "apprehensions" in a substratum are identical with it is clear, or else "an apprehension" would not be particular. But it does not follow from this that form cannot exist as different from matter, since the matter of 'apprehension" is "the receptivity of the forms ot the apprehensibles" only and is called matter *per prius* while the matter of the apprehensible is called *per posterius*.

Psychical perception is of two kinds: sensation and imagination. As said before, sensation is by nature prior to imagination for which it supplies the matter.

In short, sensation is a capacity of the body which is acted upon by the sensible. Since movements are many, sensations are also many, and because the sensibles are either common or particular, sensations are also common and particular.

(1) Cf. Ar. Text, supra, Fol. 138B, Damascus, p. 20.

(2) For either of the two, form and matter, is nature. But form is more apt to be called nature than matter; cf. Ibn Bāj. al-Samā', Fol. 8a : و كل واحد منهما (اى المادة و الصورة) طبيعة لكن الا خلق . . . ا. تكون الصورة طبيعة من المادة

(3) Cf. Ibn Bāj., Fol. 8a : و وجوده (اى الجسم الطبيعى) يتم بوجود المادة و الصورة ; Fol. 8b : فالصورة والمادة سببان لكل جسم طبيعى

(4) Since whenever we shall assume a matter that possesses a form matter shall be divisible in matter and form, and this will continue ad infinitum. This implies that 'this Verdigris', for example, will have an unlimited matter, which is absurd. Hence, matter must end at a place where it is without form; see Ibn Bāj. Fol. 7a : فانامتى وضعنا المادة ذات صورة لزم ان تكون منقسمة الى مادة و و صورة و يمر ذلك الى غير نهاية، فتكون فى هذا الز نجار سواد لانهاية لها، و هذا ايضا شنيع بل محال، فستنتهى ضرورة الى مادة غير ذات صورة،
Cf. Zeller : Aristotle, i. p. 347.

(5) Matter cannot be separated from form. This is because if it is separated it cannot exist at all. If it exists then it must be something which has matter and form : vide Ibn Bāj., Fol 7a : و ظاهر انها لاتفارق الصورة و ذلك انها ان فارقت الصور لم تكن موجودة اصلا، فان كانت موجودة لزم ان يكون شيئا ما، و عادالامر الى ان تكون ذات مادة و ليست اولى
Cf. Zeller, Aristotle, i. 349.

(6) Cf. Ibn Rushd : Talkhīs Mā Bād al-Ṭabī'ah, p. 71.

(7) Ibn Rushd uses the phrase آلة الية and gives the meaning of آلية as جسمانية, corporeal, within brackets; vide Talkhīs al-Nafs, ed, Ahwani, p. 74. He explains in Talkhīs Mā Bād al-Ṭabī'ah p. 549, that matter suffers change in so far as it is a part of the changeable, that is, when it is specifically definite, but in so far as it is matter it does not suffer change.

(8) Cf. Ibn Bāj., Fol. 8b. : كالصناعة فانه لا يمكن ان توجد الصورة الصناعية فى المادة القابلة لهاحتى تكون هى قبل موجودة و نجد ذلك فى كثير من الامور الطبيعية فان الدم لا يكون عنه جنين و تحصل فيه صورة الانسان حتى يقارنه المنى .

Arist. Phys. i. 7. 191 a 10, iv. 2.209 b 10.;
Plotinus, Ennead (tr. Mackenna), ii. p. 182: (. . . where there is decay there is a distinction between Matter and Form.).

(9) See Text, infra, Fol. 150A, Damascus, p. 80.
Cf. Arist. Phys. i. 7. 190 b 25; 191 a 10; iii. 6. 207 a 25; iv. 2.209 b9.

(10) Since there will be no 'up' and 'down', there will be no motion; cf. Ibn Baj. Fol. 12a : و ايضا فلا تكون حركة اذ لايكون فوق ولا اسفل :

(11) Cf. Arist. Phys. i. 7. 191a 10.

(12) A substratum is indispensable, because without a substratum no contraries can exist; Cf. Arist. Phys. i. 7. 191a 15; also Plotinus, (Mack.), ii. p. 202.

(13) Ibn Bāj. in Fol. 144b says that if anything comes to it it will set it in motion; (و كذا ان ورد وارد حركه فوروده حركة)

(14) Mover is of two kinds: not-homogeneous, e. g., the mover of the spherical bodies, and homogeneous. Cf. Ar. Text p. 59. also p. 65.

(15) Zeller in his Aristotle, i. p. 342, says: "All becomes that which it comes to be out of its opposite. What becomes warm must before have been cold."

(16) Cf. Arist. Phys. iv. 9. 217 a 22.
Ibn Bāj. further explains that fire cannot be cold but in so far as it is fire, and not in so far as it is body; vide Fol. 36a: فان النار لايمكن ان تكون باردة لكن من اجل انها نار لا من اجل انها جسم .

(17) For example, the beginning and the end of a straight line are contrary to each other; vide Ibn Bāj. Fol. 63a و ليس كذلک في الخط المستقيم لان ما منه غير ما اليه بالموضوع، فان طرف ا غير طرف ب.

Cf. Arist. Phys. viii. 8. 264 b 14 sq.; Ibn Rushd: al-Sam', Hyd. P 61

(18) A straight line is incomplete and essentially limited. It is only completed by something else. Similarly, a

rectilinear motion is imperfect and not complete; it is completed by something contrary to motion, viz. rest. Hence, it has two extremes—starting point, finishing point,--and a middle point; vide Ibn Bāj.

والخط المستقيم ناقص عنه محدود بذاته، و انما يتم بشئ خارج عنه،
Fol. 63 a : و كذلک الحرکة المستقيمة ناقصة غير تامة و انما يتممها
شئ اخر غيرها و هوالسکون...فهي اول و اخر و وسط.

Cf. Arist. Phys., viii. 9. 265 a 28.

(19) Cf. Ibn Bāj., Fol 23 a: و لما کان المتصل ضرورة ذا اجزاء

(20) For the terms اقل, few, and اکثر, many, are used for what is numerical, and the terms اعظم, great and اصغر, small, for what has contiguity; vide Ibn Bāj. Fol. 38b:

فان الاقل و الاکثر فيماله عدد والاعظم والاصغر فيماله اتصال
also Fol. 39 a : ان کل متناسبتين فبينهما ضرورة معنى واحدا بعينه
مشترک يقبل الاقل والاکثر.

Cf. Arist. Phys., viii. 8. 264 b 34.

(21) For when mover and moved are bodies then the movement of the moved is necessarily unnatural. Now, if either of them is first to the other, then either of the two moves the other, but the mover must exceed in power, as that is why it causes motion. Since the mover suffers motion from the moved, it gets tired through moving it, for there is difference between the weariness of the mover due to setting the moved in motion and the weariness which it suffers from itself; vide Ibn Bāj. Fol. 42 a:

لان المحرک و المتحرک اذا کانا جسمين فانالمتحرک ضرورة حرکته عنه
غير طبيعية، فان کان کلو احد منهما عند صاحبه اولا، فکلواحد منهما
يحرک صاحبه غير انالمحرک تفضل قوته و لذلک يحرک و لانه
يتحرک عنالمتحرک لذلک يکل عن تحريک المتحرک، فان فرقابين
کلال المحرک عن تحريکه المتحرک و بين کلاله اللاحق له من ذاته ـ

Cf. F. Rahman: Avicenna's Psychology, p. 141, 58.

(22) Cf. Ibn Bāj., Fol. 42 a : و لذلک ليست ايضا تستمرالنسبة بين
المحرک والمتحرک ـ

(23) Cf. Poltinus: Enneads. ii. (mack.), p. 182-6. Plato does not seem to have said so in Timaeus.

(24) Matter's natural inclination or longing for form has been described by Zeller in his Aristotle, i. p. 392.

(25) Cf. Arist. Met. o. ix. 8. 1050 a 15.

(26) Cf. Arist. Met. H. viii. 1045 b 21.

(27) Everything has an inherent longing in its nature; Ibn Bāj. Fol. 54 a كلو احد من هذه فتشوقه بالطبع غريزة فيه

That matter owns a natural inclination or longing for form has been explained by Aristotle; cf. De Geneet Cor. ii. 10. 336 b 4; Zeller: Arist. i. p. 379. ; Ibn Rushd : T'abiāh, p. 136.

(28) Cf. Aris. Met. K. xi. 1060 a 20; 107 = b 12; I07IaIo; 1042 a 27.

(29) Form and matter are correlated, and the being of form is the actuality of what is potential. "Matter", as Zeller explains, " is in itself or in its capacity that where of Actuality is From; and consequently Matter of itself the implies Form. . . . On the other hand Form is that which gives completeness to Matter by realising its potential capacities; it is the Energy or Entelechy of Matter." (Arist. i. p. 379).

(30) That is, matter and from are different in their essence only, since the material qua material is mere potentiality which has not yet in any respect arrived at 'actuality.'

(31) Matter does not at all exist as separated from form. It is always connected with it; and its being in contact with a form is no change, since matter, in assuming a form, suffers either generation or destruction. Cf. Text, supra, Note No. 9. p. 42 ; Zeller, Arist. i. p. 382.

(32) Cf. Text, infra, Fol. 149 B, Damascus, p. 79

(33) Matter through its relation with the first from imitates that which is actual, and so it moves and assumes another form. This is because 'matter' is not at all a thing in actuality, and is necessary for it to be a 'thing' when moves to be connected with another form. Cf. Text, Fol 152B, Damascus, p. 90.

also Arist. De Gen. Et Cor. ii. 9. 335 b. 17; b30; Zeller: Arist. i. 383.

(34) Form or actuality is at rest, since it does not suffer motion, but ceases to be and comes to be without suffering change in its essence either by becoming or by decaying : vide Ibn Bāj, Fol. 221 a 3 : فلذلک يقال انها (الصورة) ساكنة لا نها لا تتحرک بل تعدم و توجد، لا يتغير ذاتها لا بکون و لا فساد

Cf. Arist. Phys. v. I. 224 b 25.

(35) Cf. Text, Fol. 153A : وهى غيرذات ذجزاء, Damascus, p. 92.

(36) See note 34 (c.iii.)

Ibn Bājjah explains that form has no motion, because it is no bodies, and if it suffers, it does so accidentally, such as when a grammarian moves, they say, "grammar is moving"; cf. Fol. 221 a : و هذه الصورة فلا تتحرک لانها ليست اجساما بل ان تحرکته فبالعرض كما يقال فى النحو انه متحرک اذا تحرک النحوى.

(37) That the existent is divided into لذاته ' essential, and لغيره accidental, is also evident from the following: fol. 220 b: والنبات فليس من الموجوات لذاتها ، بل من الموجودات لغيرها من الاجسام .

(38) Cf. Arist. Phys. vii. I. 242. b 24.

(39) Cf. Text, Fol. 149A, Damascus, p. 76. p. 58. 2.

(40) Ibn Bājjah obviously refers to Phys. VIII and the sixteenth book of Animals, but 'continuity', so far as I have understood, has not been discussed by Aristotle in either place in the way Ibn Bāj. has dealt with here. The only thing which Aristotle says in Phys. VIII and on which, probably, Ibn Bājjah has based his theory is "everything that is essentially in motion is continuous" (5. 257 b I). See also Phys. iii. I. 200 b 7 where he says, "Now motion is supposed to belong to the class of things which are continuous"; ibid iv. II. 218 b II v. 3. 227 a 10; vi. 2. 232 b 24. For his reference to the book of Animals see Der Portibus Animalium, ii. 9. 654 b 14. in his al-Samā' (fol. 64 a), towards the end of the eighth book, Ibn Bāj. speaks of the eternity of the existence of the thing moved by the First Mover. He further describes that the cause of its eternity is its connection with its

principle, which is the First and accompanies it in existence eternally, since He is in it and has connection with it ; وبين ان المتحرك عن مثل هذا المحرك (اى الاول) دائم الوجود، و سبب دوام وجوده اتصاله بمبدأه، ومبدأه اول و هويرفده دائما بالوجود لانه فيه و متصل به -

(41) The Arab philosophers usually refer to the two treatises of Aristotle, viz. De Caelo and De Mundo, as kitāb al-Samā' wa' l-'Alam.

(42) Cf. Arist. De Cae. iii. I. 298 a 30; De Mun. 2. 391 b 9.

(43) Ibn Bāj. obviously refers to the passage of Risāla Fi 'l-'Aql, (ed. Bouyges, p. 30) wherein al-Fārābi raises this question " If the forms that are in the Actual Intellect and are separated from matter can exist without matter, then what is the necessity of assuming them to be in matter? And, how do they descend from so perfect a being to an imperfect being?" Al-Fārābi tries to answer this question and suggests " Some one may answer : this is being done so only to make matter perfect in its being." But he, later on, adds, "this implies that form has come into being for the sake of matter only—this is contrary to what Aristotle holds." Now what Ibn Bāj. claims to have made clear here is that, since cause, in so far as it is an end, is an entelechy, it necessarily exists in a substratum, for the elements for which it has come to be are also in a substratum. So the existence of forms in a substratum is the cause of the being of the elements in a substratum, elements and forms being called bodies *pet prius et posterius*.

(44) Ibn Bāj. has never clearly said, in this book, that matter exists for the sake of form, but what he said concerning the relation of matter and form on Fol. 164B, Damascus, p. 64, may be quoted to support this view. Aristotle is also not precise in this concern ; cf. Phys. iii. 7. 207 ; 7. 191a 10 ; 9. 192a 22.

(45) This is evidently understood from what Ibn Bāj. says, " the souls of the animal precede in time the substances

that are intelligible in term, and the intelligible substances are most suitable for this term ;" (fol. 221a9 : و انفس الحيوان تتقدم بالزمان الجواهر المعقولة فى الاسم و الجواهر المعقولة هى اخلق فى الوجود بهذا الاسم.

(46) Cf. zeller : Arist. ii. p. 338. 5.

(47) Cf. Arist De An. i. 1. 403 a 16.

(48) Cf. Arist. Met. viii. 6. ch. 28. 1024 b 3 ; Zel. : Aris. i. p. 220 ft.

(49) Cf. Zeller : Arist. i. p. 351.

(50) Ibn Baj. refers to the following passage of al-Fārabi's Risala fi'l-'Aql, ed. Bouyges, p. 17 : فاذا حصلت المعقولات بالفعل صارت حينئذ احد موجودات العالم و عدت من حيث هى معقولات فى جملة الموجودات،

This passage obviously indicates that the " intelligible being " is different from the material being. Ibn Bāj. makes the matter more clear when he describes that the common sense does not exist in itself, but after having been perceived it becomes a definite thing and an existent of the universe ; (cf. fol. 220 b : فاذا انما يعطى المنى المادة قوة الحس المشترك فيماله ذلك و ليس هو فى نفسه شيئا موجودا، و اذا احس صار شيئا مشاراليه واحد موجودات العالم و اذا كان بحيث يبقى فيه رسوم ما احس بعد غيبة المحسوس صار بالفعل شيئا مشارا اليه و صار احدالموجودات فى العالم.

(51) Cf. Text, Fol. 153A, Damascus, p. 92.

(52) Cf. Arist. Met. 1010 a 15 ; Phys. viii. 3. 253 b 9 sqq.

(53) Cf. Text, Fol. 148A, Damascus, pp. 70 & 71.

(54) Different grades of existence have elaborately been discussed by Ibn al-Sīd al-Batalyawsi, a friend and contemporary of Ibn Baj., in his Kitab al-Hada'iq , in the end of his discussion he mentions " the far and the near grades of existence", vide al-Andalus, vol. v. 1940, p. 64.5

(55) Cf. Arist. Phys. iii. 4. 204 b 32.

(56) See note Ch. ii. 54.

(57) As explained by Ibn al-Sīd in his Ḥadā'iq (al-Andalus. vol. v. 1940 p. 65. 8) the first existent generated by God is the nine existents called al-Thawāni (the secondary beings) and "the intellect abstracted from matter". These are followed in existence by the ' intellect ' entrusted to with the world of the elements and is called " The Active Intellect ", like the *thawani*, it is abstracted from matter and has been regarded as the tenth stage.

(58) Cf. Ibn Bāj. fol. 54 a : واما الحيوان فانه كما قيل فى مواضع كثيرة بالطبيعة يغتذى -

(59) That is, this faculty of sense-perception does not originate by necessity, but sensation and imagination originate for the sake of the reasoning faculty.

(60) Cf. Ibn Rushd : Ṭ. al-Nafs, ed. Ahwāni, p. 73. 16. Hyd, p. 67.

(61) Cf. Text. infra, Fol. 164A, Damascus, p. 145.

(62) Cf. Text supra, Fol. 147B, Damascus, p. 69.

(63) Cf. Arist. De An. ii. 5. 417 a 6 ; 417 a 12 , ' 22 sqq ; also Ibn Rushd : Ṭalkhīṣu al-Nafs, ed. Ahwāni, p. 20. 2, Hyd. 17.

(64) Cf. Arist. De An. ii. 5. 417 a 30 ; b 19, 30 ; 418 a 1 ; Ibn Rushd, Nafs. p. 20.

(65) Cf. Ibn Rushd, Nafs, Ahwāni, p. 25 Hyd. p. 22. 10.

(66) See Text supra, Fol. 143A, Damascus, p. 45. note 6 (ch. II).

(67) Cf. Arist. De An. ii. 5. 416 b 33 ; De Somno. i. 454 a 9.

(68) See Text, Fol. 147B, Damascus, p. 69.

(69) See Text, Fol. 146 A & B, Damascus, pp. 63, 64.
Cf. Ibn Rushd, T. al-Nafs, Ahwāni. p. 21. 2, Hyd. p. 17-18.

(70) Cf. Ibn Rushd, ,, ,, p. 73. 16, Hyd. p. 68. 19.

(71) Ibid ,, ,, ,, p. 74. 1, Hyd. p. 69 5.

(72) See Text, Fol. 146B, Damascus, p. 65.

(73) This specific form which moves the species is, as described by Ibn Bāj. in Tadbīr, p. 68, called nature or the like. For a thirsty person, for example, finds in his soul a spiritual form of water, and a hungry man, that of food, and so on. That which is like nature, e. g. the lover finds the form of the beloved.

(74) See Text, Fol. 146B, Damascus, p. 64.

(75) Cf. Text, Fol. 147B & 153A, Damascus, pp. 70 and 95, respectively.

(76) A similar argument has been used by Ibn Bāj. for the problem whether 'spiritual forms' can exist separately from bodies. He holds that they cannot exist as separable, otherwise many absurdities would follow—one of their is the existence of the definite individuals before their existence, see fol. 221 a & b : ولووجدت (اى الصور الروحانية) مفارقة للزم احد امرين اما ان يكون اجساما و لذلك تتصل بالاجسام و كونها ، اجسام ، محال، و ايضا فلو كانت موجودة مفارقة للزم من ذلك ايضا محالات كثيرة...و هو وجود اشخاص الاعراض مفارقة لان هذه الاعراض هي التي تحرك فيلزم ما يلزم و هو وجودالاشخاص قبل وجودها.

(77) Cf. Zeller : Arist. ii. p. 58. 6 ; (De An. ii. 5. init.)

(78) Cf. Arist. De An. ii. 5. 416 b 33 ; 417 a 13.

(79) Cf. Arist. De Motu. 703 a 25 ; De Caelo. 269 a 2, 29. Ibn Bāj. Fol. 94 b : قال ارسطو عند ما عدد الاسطقسات في الثانية عشر من الحيوان

(80) Cf. Ibn Bāj. Fol. 93 b : انواع التركيب ثلثة : الاول تركيب الاسطقسات- و هو من الصورة و المادة الاولى، والثانى التركيب من الاسطقسات و هو في المتشابه الاجزاء، والثالث التركيب من هذه و هي الاعضاء في ذى الا عضاء و اجزاء النبات كاليد و الرجل وما جانسهما.

(81) Cf. Arist. De Gen. et Cor. i. 5. 322 a 32.
In al-'Athar fol. 68 b, Ibn Bāj., however, explains that all that is compound is composed of the four elements. Composition takes place sometimes by way of تجاوز (exceeding into each other) and sometimes by way of مزج mixing, : و كان كل مركب فمن بسايط اربعة و كان تركيبها على طريق التجاوز و قد يكون على طريق المزج.

(82) Cf. Arist. De Gen. et Cor. i. 6. 322 b 10.

(83) Cf. Arist. ibid. ; i. 10. 328 b 15-25.

(84) Cf. Arist. Meteo. iv. 2. 379 b 12 ; ' 25-30 ; 380 a 5, 11 sq.

(85) Cf. Arist. Meteo. iv. 2. 379 b 8.

(86) Cf. Ibn Bāj. Fol. 82 b : و كل فاعل و منفعل و هيولاهما مشتركة فهما متضادان ضرورة فلذلك كلو احد منهما يحركه صاحبه و يتحرك، والفعل والانفعال لا يكون حتى يماس و قد يكون اختلاط وقد لا يكون. Cf. Arist. De Gen., et Cor. i. 6. 322 b 22 sq ; 10. 327b 23 sq.

(87) Ibn Bāj. differentiates between the terms تكون generation, and امتزاج, mixing, Generation is caused either by one element or by many elements, and that by decomposing the capacity of that element or of either. In mixing, however, the powers of the elements remain in actuality but, because their extremes having been decomposed, they develop into an intermediary power which mixes them as long as they are in mutual contact. Thus they produced a new being, a different form, or many forms corresponding to the different sorts of combination and alteration followed by different kinds of generation ; vide Fol. 76 b : ان كل متكون فهو من اسطقس ا ومن اكثر من اسطقس فان الاسطقس الواحد انما يتكون، عنه اسطقس غيره كالنار تتولد منه ساير الثلاثة كما قيل فى كتاب الكون والفساد، و اما من اثنين فقد يكون منهما اسطقس اخر كما قيل فى كتاب الكون، و ذلک اذا فسد المجتمع بفساد قوة احد هما، و اما اذا فسدت النهايات و بقيت القوى بالفعل لكن ليست خالصة بل حدث فيها قوة مركبة متوسطة و ذلک ماداما مختلطين فعند ذلک يحدث عنهما موجودا اخر و صورة اخرى و يمكن ان يحدث فى هذه صور كثيرة بضروب من .الاستحالة تتبعها ضروب من التكونات.

(88) Cf. Arist. Meteo. iii. 6. 378 a 18 sq.

(89) See Text, Fol. 152 B, Damascus, p. 91.

(90) Cf. Arist. Meteo. iv. 10, 388 a 13 sq.

(91) Cf. Arist. Ibid. i. 397 b 5.

(92) See Text, Fol. 147 B, Damascus, 69 ; p.Arist. Met. ix. 1050 a 15.

(93) For matter in every body necessarily needs a form for its existence ; vide Text, Fol. 147 B, Damascus, p. 68.

(94) Form thus suffers change necessarily by accident; vide Text, Fol. 147 B, Damascus, p. 68.

(95) For matter itself is the essence or substratum of the form.

(96) These material states have obviously been alluded to by Aristotle in the following: Meteo. iv. 2. 379 b 12: "the concoction is due to heat; its species are ripening, boiling, broiling . . . "; ibid, ' 25: " In some cases of concoction the end of the process is the nature of the thing—nature, that is, in the sense of the formal cause and essence, . . . ".

(97) Aristotle nowhere in Phys. VIII says that the mover cannot be without circular movement. But he establishes an infinite motion that is single and continuous, and maintains that this motion is rotatory motion; see Phys. VIII, p. 8.

Referring to the continuous motion Ibn Bāj. in his commentary on the eighth chapter of the Physics, fol. 63b, explains that some sort of this motion is available in the heavenly motion, and that this motion is accidental and is caused by something else; (والحركة التى يذكرها ارسطو فى هذه المقالة الثامنة حين يقول الا ان (بعض هذه توجد فى الحركةالسماوية وهى الحركة بالعرض من غير.)

Cf. Arist. De Caelo. i. 2.269 a 7.

(98) Cf. Arist. Meteo. iv. 2.379 b 18.

(99) Cf. Arist. De Gen. An. ii. 3736 b 22 sq.; 737a 9; Phys. vii 3. 247 b I; De An. i. 3.407 a 33.

(100) Otherwise, matter is " merely unrealised form, in the potentiality of which form is the actuality, see Zeller: Arist. ii. p. 339.

(101) Text, Fol. 149 B, Damascus, p. 79.

(102) "Change", Ibn Bāj. says, " is always followed by change, since 'this change', for instance, descends on the supposed change fol. 64a: والتغير سيتبعه تغير اذ ينزل هذا التغير منزلةالتغير المفروض , فيكون قبل كل تغير مفروض تغير يتقدم fol. 57a: من ذلک النوع: Cf. Arist. Phys. viii 2.252 b 9.

(103) Arist. says everything that changes must be divisible; see Phys. vi. 4.234 b 10.

(104) Cf. Text, Fol. 147 B, Damascus, p. 70.

(105) See Text, Fol. 149 A, Damascus, p. 76.

(106) See Text, Fol. 143 A, Damascus, p. 45.

(107) See Text, Fol. 146 A, and 150 B, Damascus, p. 63 & 83, respectively.

(108) See Text, Fol. 150 B, Damascus, p. 83.

(109) Ibn Sīnā, however describes the distinction between الصورة and المعنى as follows: (Shifā', Fol. 182 b II) وقد جرت العادة بان يسمى مدرک الحس صورة ومدرک الوهم معنى .

(110) Ibn Sīnā explains apprehension precisely as follows: " It seems that every apprehension is to grasp the form of the apprehensible in a certain manner. Now if apprehension is concerned with a material thing, then it is to grasp its form separately from matter. But the kinds of separation are various and of different grades. For the immattered form, due to its matter, suffers states and attributes that essentially do not belong to the form in so far as it is 'that definite form'. Sometimes, therefore, form is separated from matter but remains in contact with all or some of these conditicns; sometimes it is completely separated — this is so by separating form from matter as well as from the attributes that it acquires through the matter. See Shīfa, Fol. 163b 9:
يشبه ان يكون كل ادراک هوا اخذ صورة المدرک بنحو من الانحاء فان كان الادراک ادرا کا لشئی مادی فهوا خذ صورته مجردة عن المادة تجريدا ما ، الا ان اصناف التجريد مختلفته ، و مراتبها متفاوتة ، فان الصورة المادية يعرض لها بسبب المادة احوال وامور ليست هى لها بذاتها من جهة ماهى تلک الصورة ، فتارة يكون النزع عن المادة نزعا مع تلک العلايق كلها او بعضها ، و فتارة يكون النزع نزعا کا ملا وذلک بان يجرد المادة وعن اللواحق التى لها من جهة المادة .

(111) That is, things are from the mover or they are caused by the mover. Ibn Bāj. perhaps refers to what he has said that the art proceeds from the mover (cf. Text, Fol. 139 A),

or to what he has explained about the function of the moving faculty that it makes essentially something from its own species and accidentally something else (cf. Text, Fol. 144 B, Damascus, p. 53), however, in either case things are caused by the moving faculty. But in this book he never says in so many words that things are caused by the mover.

(112) Obviously Ibn Bājjah refers to the beginning of this chapter where he explains that matter is actually neither separable from form, nor can form in a definite body be actually separated from matter (cf. Text, Fol. 140 A).

(113) Cf. Text, Fol. 143 A, Damascus, p. 44.

(114) In the philosophical terminology *Rūḥani*, an adjective from *Rūḥ*, indicates substances that are, therefore, forms of bodies and not bodies; this term is not pure Arabic and has come into use in Arabic in a group of words that is used against the usual form, since according to the Arabic syntax the usual form, would be *Rūhī* ; cf. Tadbīr ed. Asin, p. 18.

(115) Ibn Rushd describes 'sensitive forms' as divisible with the division of the matter, in the sense that through it 'the mixing forms' are divided, and hence, they can receive to contraries together, the small and the big in one and the same state; see T. al-Nafs, ed. Ahwani, p. 74.6 Hyd. p. 69.10.

(116) See note 18, Chapter IV.

(117) Cf. Arist. Phys., vi. 4 234 b 10.

(118) Cf. Arist. DE An., ii. 7.418 a 15 sq.; I'bn Rushd : T. al-Nafs, p. 27, Hyd p. 23.

(119) Cf. Arist. De Gen. An. i. 23. 731 a 30. sq.

(120) See Text, Fol. 150 A, Damascus, p. 80.

CHAPTER IV

DISCOURSE ON SIGHT

In this chapter Ibn Bājjah describes the soul as the first entelechy and designates vision as the first entelechy of the eye. The soul of vision is located in the vitreous humour in the eye and perceives colour, its first sensible.

Colour can be perceived only through the medium of air which serves the eye through light alone, for in darkness colour exists potentially.

That which gives light is illuminating *per prius et posterius-per prius* as e.g. the sun and fire, *per posterius* as e.g. the moon and transparent bodies. Light is the sensation in the air caused by the presence of a body, and it makes the transparent body visible.

Thus, the illuminating has a relation and position to the transparent, each part of the illuminating having a relation to each part of the transparent.

Colour moves the transparent only in so far as it is received. Since colour possesses shape, sight perceives shape, length and all that is necessary for colour. As causes are either essential or accidental, the objects of vision are either essential or accidental.

(1) See Ar. Text, Fol. 139 B, 140 A, Damascus, p. 28.

(2) Aristotle explains that everything is said to be what it really is in virtue primarily of its form, and only secondarily in virtue of its matter ; cf. De An. ii. 2. 414 a 9-13; also see note 38 (Chap. I).

(3) For iron *per se* is not diaphanous. It becomes mirror only after being polished.

(4) That an embryo has vegetative soul is clear from the following words of Ibn Bāj. (Fol. 216 b/Risālat al-Ittiṣāl, Al-Andalus, vol. vii. 1942 p. 12) ; و ذلک فی الزمان الذی یحتوی علیه الرحم، فانه یتخلق اولا فاذا کمل تخلقه اغتذی و نمی.

(5) See Ar. Text, Fol. 155 A, Damascus, p. 99.

(6) Cf. Arist. Meteo. iv. 12. 390 a 10 ; De An. ii. 1. 412 b 12-21 ; 8. 420 b 1 ; De Gen. Anim. ii. 1. 735 a 8.

(7) Ibn Bāj. perhaps rightly assigns the faculty of vision to the vitreous humour inasmuch as the vitreous humour has been regarded by Greek Physicians as the organ of vision (see Meyerhof : Ten treatises on the Eye ascribed to Ḥunayn Ibn Isḥāq, p. 120, واما الة البصر و هى الرطوبة الجليدية Ibn Sīna locates this faculty in the concave nerve (see F. Raḥmān : Avicenna's Psychology (MS.), p. 6 ; also Shifā, Bodl. Poc. 125, fol. 160 b : فمنها البصر و هى قوة مرتبة فى العصبة المجوفة تدرك صورة ما ينطبع فى الرطوبة الجليدية من اشباح الاجسام .

But Ḥunayn explains, the capacity of vision flows from the brain through the concave nerve ; cf. كتاب العشر مقالات فى العين المنسوب لحنين. ed, Meyerhof under the title 'Ten treatises on the Eye of Ḥunayn, p. 120 : و اما قوة البصر .فانها تنبعث من الدماغ فى العصبة المجوفة .

(8) Cf. Arist. De An. ii. 7. 419a 13 ; 11. 423 b 20.

(9) Aristotle does not say that air serves the eye, but he says that air and water are transparent because they contain a certain substance—the activity of this substance being light. Light is as it were the proper colour of what is transparent. Cf. De An. ii. 7. 418 b 1-12.

(10) Aristotle describes the arising of a variety of colours when the sun is beheld through fog or cloud of smoke, as though in itself it appears white but takes a crimson hue ; cf. De Sensu, 3. 440 a 7.

Ibn Rushd is very near to Ibn Bāj. in his expression ; cf. T. K. al-Nafs, ed. Ahwani, p. 33, Hyd. p. 29.

(11) Ibn Rushd obviously follows Ibn Bāj. in dividing the illuminant into two, *per prius et posterius* ; cf. T.K. al-Nafs, ed. Ahwani, p. 31, Hyd. p. 27. Aristotle, however, is not clear about this division, but refers to the influence of fire or " something resembling ' the uppermost body' ". Perhaps this " uppermost body " has been expressed by Ibn Rushd in the phrase الجسم الالهى, and, as quoted by Ahwani in his ft. note, by Thomas Acquinas as "corpori coelesti". Ibn Bajjah makes this expression quite clear when he uses الشمس; cf. De An. ii. 7. 418 b 12.

(12) Cf. Arist. De An. ii. 7. 419 a 3. In his expression Ibn Rushd is very near to Ibn Bāj., see T. K. al-Nafs, ed. Ahwani, p. 31, Hyd. 27.

(13) Cf. Arist. De An. ii. 7. 419 a 1-5; Ibn Rushd : T. Nafs, ed. Ahwani, p. 32, Hyd. 27.

(14) Aristotle discusses the causes of ' Shooting-stars ', the phenomena of combustion, and the nature of comets and the milky-way ' in Meteorology, i. 5-6. 342 b 22 sq.

(15) Cf. Arist. De Gen. An. iii. 11. 761 b 20.

(16) This hemistich belongs to a panegyric composed by Abū Nuwās in praise of the famous bermekide vizir Ja'far Ibn Yaḥyā. The complete verse is as follows :

ذاک الوزیر الذی طالت علاوته * کانه ناظر فی السیف بالطول

see K. al-Wuzarā' wal-Kuttāb by Abū Abdullah Muḥammad Ibn Abdrus al-Jahshayāri, ed. Mustafa al-Saqqā, Ibrāhīm al-Abyari and Abdul Ḥafiz Chalbi, 1938, Egypt. p. 215.

(17) Probably a work of Ibn Bājjah on Mathematics apparently lost.

(18) Ibn Bājjah tries to explain his phrase تابع لتغیر in Samā',Fol. 29 b. " the change that occurs in ' relations ' is not change, but is a necessary consequence of change, and hence, it exists in the ' now ' ; and similar is its passing away "; ویکون للنسب تغیر تابع لتغیو فلذلک یکون فی الان وکذلک فسادها

(19) The term الان , according to Ibn Bājjah means the end of motion ; cf. fol. 29 a : ففی الان الذی هو منتهی الحرکة . But it also indicatees the end of rest and the beginning of motion, or the end of motion and the beginning of rest ; vide fol. 29 b : الان الذی هو نهایة السکون و مبدأ الحرکة او نهایة الحرکة و مبدأ السکون .

(20) This is obviously based on the Aristotelian statement that the positions and the character of the motion of animals are ' abnormal ' ; see Phys. viii. 4. 254 b 23.

(21) Ibn Bājjah perhaps refers to some of his independent discourse on the reflection of light which is lost. He does not discuss this problem in K. al-Nafs.

(22) Cf. Arist. De Sensu iii. 440 b 1-18 ; 439 b 11 ; De An. ii. 7. 419 a 14.

(23) Arist. refers to Democritus' view in his De An. ii. 7. 419a 15.

(24) Arist. De An. ii. 7. 419 a 9.

(25) Ibid ; 419 a 21 ; also Text, Fol. 155 B, Damascus, p. 102.

(26) المرايا plural of المرءة, mirror.

(27) Cf. Ar. Text, Fol. 154 A, Damascus, p. 97.

CHAPTER V

DISCOURSE ON HEARING

The faculty of hearing is the entelechy of the sense of hearing and its function is to apprehend the reverberating impression caused in the air by the impact of two bodies mutually impinging upon each other. This being so, the impinging bodies must be hard enough to produce sound.

When the air in the ear-hole reverberates immensely so much so that the sound caused by one impact lasts long till the next impact takes place, the sound turns into a musical note.

Since air is the first recipient of sound, the impinging and the impinged bodies are perceived accidentally, and hence, error occurs in this sense.

Some bodies produce sound — these bodies possess soul and an organ for making sound — and some do not produce sound and possess no soul.

Since sense-perception concerns "the form" of the sensible, the sense of hearing concerns the form that is in air and water and does not care for shape, and the like, that does not constitute sound.

(1) Sound, according to Aristotle, may mean either (a) actual or (b) potential sound. Actual sound is generated by an impact, and so there must be a body impinging and a body impinged upon ; what sounds does so by striking against something else; cf. Arist. De An. ii. 8. 419 b 5- 13.

(2) The equivalent of رطب in this concern is not found in the works of Aristotle who, however, says, "not all bodies can by impact on one another produce sound; impact on wool makes no sound, while the impact on bronze or any body which is smooth and hollow does". Cf. De An. ii. 8. 419 b 14-15.

(3) Cf. Arist. De An. 8. 419 b 23; Ibn Rushd: T. al-Nafs, Ahwani, p. 35.

(4) Cf. Arist. De An. ii. 8. 419b 18-20.

(5) i. e. sound is an impression which is set in motion by the the air in which the impression takes place.

(6) Cf. Arist. De An. ii. 8. 419 b 26; 420 a 4.

(7) In his Kitāb al-Nafs Ibn Bāj. does not precisely say that the eye commits mistakes.

(8) Arist. De An. ii, 8. 420 b 5.

(9) Aristotle mentions the sound caused accidentally by saying: " The fish, like those in the Achelous, which are said to have voice, really make the sounds with their gills or some similar organ", (De An. ii. 8. 420 b 11).

Ibn Bājjah seems to have differed from Aristotle when he explains that the sound made by such animal as cricket is due to the coming out of the air. Nevertheless, he agrees with Aristotle in so far as respiration is concerned, inasmuch as 'breathing out' prerequisites 'breathing in'. Cf. Arist. De An. ii. 8. 420 b 15; also Hist. An. iv. 9. 535 a 27-536 b 24, where the cricket or cicada has been mentioned. Ibn Rushd follows Ibn Bājjah; see T. al-Nafs, Ahwani, p. 38.

CHAPTER VI

DISCOURSE ON SMELL

The sense of smell is located in the nose; and it apprehends the "form" of the object of smell.

The first object of smell is odour which is essentially in every mixed body.

This sense is strong in the animals and weak in man. Those animals that possess lungs do not smell unless they breathe, for this sense has a covering which is withdrawn when "inhaling" takes place.

Since "mixing" prerequisites "broiling" which is caused by con-natural heat when it acts in moist and dry bodies, smell prerequisites a second mixing in course of which the wet washes the qualitative dry.

Some odorous things are manifest in scent and smell without fire or heat, e.g.musk, others are not so and require heat, e.g. the aromatic wood, and red arsenic.

This sense does not apprehend any quality of the object of smell without flavour.

(1) This work of Alexander of Aphrodisias was rendered into Arabic by Abu 'Uthmān-al-Dimashqi, A unique MS. exists in the Escurial Library No. 794 (vide Casiri: Bibliotheca Arabic-Hispana Escurialensis, vol. I. p. 242, Foll. 69b-7Ia). I tried to get the photostats of the MS. but was refused on the plea that Father Morata is working on it.

But here Ibn Bāj. refers to one of his own writings containing, 'مقالة الاسكندر فى اللون و اى شئى هو على راى ارسطو' included in the Berlin MS which is now lost ; see Ahlwardt: Die Handschriften, . . . vol. iv. No. 5060.

(2) This view is obviously supported by Ibn Rushd, cf. T. al-Nafs. ed. Ahwani. p. 39, Hyd. p. 34.

(3) Cf. Arist. De Sensu, 5.443b24 sq. ; 444bI-I4; '30-445a.

(4) Cf. Arist. De An. ii. 9.421a 9.

(5) Cf. Arist. De An. ii. 7.419b ٢.

(6) Cf. Arist. De An. ii. 8.420b 23; De Sensu, 5.444b1 sq.

(7) This is the case with all other senses that they do not perceive what is in immediate contact with the organ of sense. See De An. ii. 9.421b 14-19; also K. al-Nafs, ed. Ahwani, p. 151. 11 also Pers. MS Fol. 47 a 20 : و این حواس دیگر راکه وصف کردیم نه چنین باشد که آن حواس تا در هوا درمیان نباشد محسوسات خرد را نیابد ، چون حس بینائی و شنوائی و بو یائی که اگر مردم چیز دیدنی را برحدقه چشم نهد نه بیند و اگر چیز آواز دهنده بر درون گوش نهد آواز آن نتواند شنید و اگر چیز بویا را ظاهر مجرای بینی نهد بوی آن نیابد .

(8) For Aristotle it remains a problem whether there is such 'curtain' or covering which is drawn back in inhalation. He thinks that probably the organ of smell has something like covering just as man's eyes have in the eyelids a kind of shelter or envelope, (De An. ii. 9.421b 29-422a 4). Ibn Bājjah however categorically states that it has a curtain. This is perhaps for the fact that Aristotle in the De Sensu (5.444b 21-25) says "when the creatures which respire are respiring the current of breath removes something that is laid like a lid upon the organ proper; while in creatures which do not respire this is always off". See also K.al-Nafs, Ahwani, p. 150 and the Pers. MS. Fol. 47 a : و اما دیگر جانوران که راه گذر بینی دارند بالای گذرگاه حجابی بود شان که هوا را باز دارد از رسیدن بدان منافذ مگر آنکه بر کشند و بجتبایند و همچنین نتوانند دید مگر که چشم بکشایند .

(9) Cf. Arist. De Sensu, 5.443a 21-30.

(10) Vide Text, Fol. 157 B, Damascus, p. 113.

(11) Aristotle explains the object of smell in De Sensu, 5.443a 7.

(12) Cf. Arist. De Sensu, 5.443a1; 'b3; 445a 14; also 4.44Ib18.

(13) Cf. Arist. Ibid. 4.441b 18; 5.443 b 16.

(14) In his expression Ibn Rushd follows Ibn Bāj. cf. T. al-Nafs, ed. Ahwāni, p. 40, Hyd. p. 34.

(15) Cf. Ibn Rushd: T. al-Nafs, ed. Ahwani, p. 40 Hyd. p. 34 34; for (المعية) and اللبنى see K.al-Nafs, ed. Ahwāni, p. 150; Pers. MS. fol. 47a6: وحس بویابیٔ همان شناسد که سوافق وخوش بود و یا مخالف و نا خوش و نتواند که بوی گل را از بوی میعه جدا کند و نه بوی صبر را از بوی سزبل که همین دانیم که بو یهای خوشت یا بو های ناخوش،

(16) Also known as العود الهندى , cf. Ibn Rushd: T. al-Nafs, ed. Ahwani, p. 40.

CHAPTER VII

DISCOURSE ON TASTE

Taste arises when the concoction of moist and dry bodies takes place. It is, therefore, neither in wet nor in dry object itself. Moisture is essential for the sense of taste— it is supplied by the uvula.

This sense is necessary for the animals and is possessed by all except those animals that have shells or are spongelike which employ the sense of touch instead.

This sense perceives flavour only and no other quality of the object of taste.

(1) Cf. Ar. Text, Fol. 159 A, Damascus, p. 118.

(2) Aristotle says that "the flavoured and tasteable body is suspended in a liquid matter" ; cf. De An. ii. I0. 422 a 10.

(3) Cf. Arist. De AN. ii. I0. 422a 18.

(4) Cf. T. al-Nafs, ed. Ahwani, p. 4I.
Ibn Rushd holds that the sense of taste, too, requires a medium which is to be found in 'fluid substance', and he urges against Alexander of Aphrodisias, who denies it, at some length and refers to Ibn Bājjah and Themistius. T. al-Nafs, ed. Ahwani, p. 41.

(5) Cf. Arist. De An. ii. 11. 422b8.

(6) Cf. Arist. De An. iii. I2. 434 b 10-24; De Sense, 1.436b 13.

CHAPTER VIII

DISCOURSE ON TOUCH

Touch is the faculty of perceiving the tangible body. Opinions differ whether it is a single faculty or many faculties in one substratum.

It is spread all over the body, and has no particular organ, its location being in flesh or the like. No animal is devoid of touch.

Since every sensation is capable of receiving contraries, touch also receives, and hence, it is moderately warm, cold, moist and dry.

Touch is possible through more than one medium which may not be natural. Whether it is flesh or in flesh is not clear, but it is connected with flesh.

Besides the five senses enumerated above there is no other sense.

(1) Ibn Bājjah is more clear in K. al-Ḥayawān, Fol. 95b ; where he says : واللمس فقد يظن به انه اصناف كثيرة ، فان اللمس هو الحار و البارد و الرطب و اليابس و الصلب و اللين ، و هذه القوة واحدة كانت او اكثر من واحدة فهى اللحم و ما جرى (fol. 96 a) مجراه ، و هذا الحس يحتاج اللحم اكثر مما يحتاج اليه غيره و لذلك كان الانسان احسن لمسا من سايرالحيوان لان اللحم فيه كثير و ليس له شعر ولا ريش و لا فلوس و لا خزف بل الجلد ،

In De An. ii. 11.422 b 18, Aristotle mentions this view and says " if touch is not a single sense but a group of senses, there must be several kinds of what is tangible."

(2) Ibn Bājjah explains clearly as follows : (Fol. 95 a) و هذه القوة (اى قوة اللمس) ليس لها موضوع منفرد كالعين للبصر و المنخر للشم و ثقب الاذن للسمع بل تجدها شايعة فى الجسد كله و مرحيطة به.

(3) Cf. Ibn Bāj. Fol 96 a و الحس منه ما هو شامل للاعضاء كاللمس و آلته اللحم او ما يقوم مقامه فسيوجد فى كل عضو له شركة فى الحس لحم ، و اما ان يكون منفردا كا الحواس الاربع.

Arist. De An. ii. 11. 422 b 20; 423 a 13.

(4) That the skin is not the first percipient, Ibn Bájjah argues, is clear by the fact that sensation in flesh without skin

is stronger than the sensation in flesh covered with skin; (fol. 96 a) : فجلد الانسان فقد يظن به انه الحاس الاول و اما انه ليس الحاس الاول (فذلک بين لان اللحم يحس دون الجلد اکثر مما يحس والجلد عليه

(5) Cf. Ibn Bāj. Fol. 87 a : ان کل واحد من هذه (اجسام اربعة) فهو جسم ملموس و ذلک معروف بنفسه و لما کانت الاجسام المشاهدة ليست البسائط بل ما کانت اقرب الی البساطيط ظن بان المعرفة بما نشاهد ليست مکتفية بنفسها علی ان تردف بالقول فنقول ان الحار و البارد و الرطب واليابس امور محسوسة فهی موجودة ، و هذا علم اول مکتف بنفسه فظاهر قريبا من ذلک انها فی موضوع واحد و ان قوام جسم و صورته من حيث هو ما هو ليست واحدة منها ، و انواع الاجسام المشاهدة فکل واحد منها فيه ضرورة اثنان من هذه الارع لا يخلو جسم منها.
Aris. De An. ii. II. 423 b 27.

(6) Cf. Arist. De An.ii. II. 424 a 7.

(7) Cf. Ibn Rushd: T. al-Nafs, ed. Ahwani, p. 46, Hyd. p. 40.

(8) Ibn Sina, in the same way, describes this sense (touch) in al-Shifā, fol. I66 a. "It seems", he says, "that the faculties of touch are many—every one of them characterising a particular contrariety—so that what perceives the contrariety between ' heavy ' and ' light ' is other than what perceivs the contrariety between 'hot ' and ' cold'. Since these are primary actions of sense-perception, every kind of these must have a particular faculty; but sinoe these faculties are spread equally over all organs, they are assumed to be a single faculty"; و يشبه ان تکون قوی اللمس قوی کثيرة کلو احد منها يختص بمضادة فيکون ما يدرک به المضادة التی بين الثقيل و الخفيف غيرالتی يدرک به المضادة التی بين الحار و البارد ،افان هذه افعال اولية و للحس يجيب ان يکون لکل جنس منها قوة خاصة الا ان هذه القوی لما انتشرت فی جميع الا لات بالسوية ظنت قوة واحدة.

(9) This is in opposition to what Aristotle says in De Sensu, 6. 445 b 12; see also De An. ii. 7. 418 b 27-30.

(10) Cf. Arist. De Sensu, vi. 446 a 21.

(11) Aristotle raises this question in De An. ii. 11. 422 b 23.

(12) Cf. K. al-Nafs, ed, Ahwani, p. 153; Pers. MS fol. 47 b 19 :
جواب گفت جاسه لمس ملموس را بمیانجی هوادر یابد لیکن هوا پوشیده بود و درین مثلی زد گفت اگر کسی دست باب فرو برد و بیرون آورد بدست سنگی را بر گیرد ناچار میان سنگ و دست آب بود لیکن پنهان از غایت لطافتش ، پس چون آب بتوسط میتواند بود میان دست و آنچه بدست گیرد بے آنکه نتوان دید از لطافت هوا سزاوار تر که در توسط پوشیده ماند که هوا از آب بسی لطیف تراست.

Ibn Rushd is more clear and like Ibn Bājjah refers to Themistius, see T. al-Nafs, ed. Ahwani, p. 50, Hyd. p. 45.

(13) Cf. Ibn Bāj. fol. 96 a: على ما نشاهد ان الحس فى اللحم ، و لايبالى . . . هل اللحم هو الحاس امر الروح الغريزى و اللحم

Arist. Hist. An. i. 489 a 24.

(14) Cf. Arist. Hist. An. i. 3. 489 a 18; De Part. An. ii. 1. 647 a 15; De An. iii. 13. 435 a 20.
Ibn Rushd: T. al-Nafs, ed. Ahwāni, p. 47, Hyd. p. 41.

(15) Cf. Ibn Rushd: T. al-Nafs, ed. Ahwani, p. 56,, Hyd. p. 51.

(16) Cf. Arist. De An. iii. 1. 424 b 24; Ibn Rushd: T. al-Nafs, Ahwani, p. 58, Hyd. p. 53.

(17) Cf. Ibn Bāj. fol. 110 b: و الاكمل هو الذى يوجد له جميع الاعضاء الافضل فان العظام فيما اعدت افضل من الشوک ، و كذلک جميع القوى ، و الانسان افضل الحيوان لانه يوجد له جميع اجزاء النفس و لما كانت اُجزاء الجسد انما هى الات نفسانية كالعروق والعضل و منها مايتم به قوام جميع جسده كالعظام فضرورة يجب حيث كانت اجزاء النفس اكثر ان يكون هناک عدد انواع الاعضاء اكثر ، و حيث كملت اجزاء النفس فهناک سكمل عدد انواع الاجزاء بالجملة ما كان منها عضو او ما كان منها شئيا حيوانيا ، و الانسان ففيه قوى النفس المشتركة ، و فيه قوى يختص بها هو وحده ، فلو كانت نفسا كما يجب ضرورة ان رستعمل آلة فكان بجب ضرورة ان يكون فى ذاالانسان نوع من الاعضاء لايو جد فى حيوان اصلا

Arist. Hist. An. i . 2 . 488b30; 486 b I8: Ibn Rushd T. al-Nafs, Ahwani, p. 58, Hyd. p. 53.

CHAPTER IX

ON COMMON SENSE

The five senses—sight, hearing, smell, taste and touch—are the five faculties of a single sense, viz., the common sense. The common sense plays the part of matter through which the forms of things become perceptible. It is through this common sense that a man judges and distinguishes different states of the perceptible and realises that every particle of an apple, for example, possesses taste, smell, colour, warmth or cold, for this faculty preserves the impressions of the sensibles which enable the five senses to apprehend the sensibles.

Besides its being the form of the innate heat, the common sense is the entelechy of the whole body, and hence, it is called soul. By becoming identical with different organs it becomes a form of the organised body, since this form is not in the body, and may be compared with the captain in the boat.

And also this faculty supplies matter for the faculty of imagination.

Now it is clear that the five senses and the common sense are the entelechies of the body and are, therefore, souls.

(1) Cf. Arist. De An. iii. 2. 4 b 11-22; Ibn Rushd : al-Nafs, ed. Ahwani. p. 54, Hyd. p. 48. Ibn Sīna also describes the common sense as a faculty to which all sensibles proceed; cf. Shifā, Fol. 182 a. بل الحس المشترک هوالقوة التی تتادی الیها المحسوسات کلها

(2) Cf. Ibn Rushd : T. al-Nafs, Ahwāni, p. 55, Hyd. p. 49.

(3) Ibn Rushd says that this example has been customarily used by the philosophers, Aristotle and his commentators, ; cf. T. al-Nafs, Ahwāni, p. 55, Hyd. p. 49.

(4) Cf. Ibn Rushd : T. al-Nafs. Ahwāni, p. 54.

(5) Cf. Arist. De An. iii. 2. 426 b 10; Ibn Rushd : T. al-Nafs, Ahawāni, p. 54.

(6) Cf. Ibn Rushd ; T. al-Nafs, Ahwāni, p. 54. Probably the first scholar to use this example is Alexander of Aphrodisias.

(7) The same argument is found in Ibn Sīna, see Shifa, Fol. 182 a 3 : فانه لولم تكن قوة واحدة تدرک الملون والملموس لما كان لنا ان نميز بينهما قائلين انه ليس هذا ذاک .

(8) Cf. Ibn Rushd : T. al-Nafs, Ahwani, p. 63, Hyd. 58.

(9) The soul in the body is like the captain in the boat. For the captain in the boat is a separable form ; cf. Ibn Baj. Fol. 60 a : فان النفس فی البدن کا لربان فی السفینة ، فان الربان فی السفینته صورة الاانها مفارقته

Cf. Arist. De An. i. 3. 406 a 6; ii. 1. 413 a 9.

(10) Cf. Text, Fol. 155 A, Damascus, p. 100

In al-Ḥayawān, fol. 95.b, Ibn Bāj. says that sense-perception is separable from motion in expression as matter is separable from form in the expression that describes its nature in relation to its causes which give rise to it, while it is in form ; (فالحس ينفرد عن الحركة بالقول كما تنفرد الهيولى من الصورة بالقول الذى يلخص به ما هى بالاسباب المقومة لها و هى فيها).

(11) i. e. when a body is present to the common sense it has a faculty, the common sense being the matter for the faculty and the faculty form for the common sense.

Cf. Ibn Sīnā, Shifa, fol. 180 a 18 : "Common sense perceives the form but does not preserve it (this opposes Ibn Baj. see Text, Damascus, p. 129.); the faculty of imagination, preserves it. The reason is that the soul which possesses the common sense keeps the form impressed from outside as long as the relation between the soul and the object of sight lasts. When the object of sight disappears the form is effaced from it and does not last long ;" فان الحس المشترک قابل للصورة لا حافظ ، و القوة الخيالية حافظة لما قبلت تلک ، و السبب فی ذلک ان الروح التى فيها الحس المشترک انما تثبت فيها الصورة الماخوذة من خارج منطبعة ماداست النسبة المذكور بينها و بين المبصر محفوظة او قريبة العهد ، فاذا غاب البصر انمحت الصورة عنها ، و لم تثبت زمانا يعتد به).

CHAPTER X

DISCOURSE ON THE FACULTY OF IMAGINATION

The faculty of imagination apprehends the 'form' of the sensibles that have either perished or ceased to stimulate the percipient. The ancient philosophers have been in disagreement as to what the nature of this faculty is; some considered this faculty as sense-perception, others made it opinion, yet others came to the conclusion that it was a combination of opinion and sense-perception. But it cannot be treated as opinion, for an opinion is held to be true by those who form an opinion, whereas sometimes imagination cannot be true. Perception needs presence o the sensible, while imagination does not, rather sometimes it deals with that which cannot be perceived—the faculty of imagination cannot, therefore, be perception either. Nor can it, for the reasons stated above, be a combination of opinion and sense-perception.

This faculty is not confined to man alone and is possessed by most animals ; and it is the noblest faculty in irrational animals.

This faculty depends upon the common sense, since it needs sensation ; and hence it perishes with the common sense. But, since it is, like an end for the common sense, it is in its being, nobler than the common sense.

It is through this faculty that the animals are, for example, moved to have progeny and look after their young ones, and their appetitive part is set in motion.

It is therefore clear that the imagining faculty is an entelechy for a natural organised body, and is therefore soul.

Besides the common sense and the faculty of imagination there cannot be a third faculty, since the existents are either material or abstract—that which is material is the specific body, and that which is abstract is the imaginative faculty which is like perfume in between the existents that are separated from matter and those that are material.

(1) Cf. Arist. De An, iii. 3. 427 a 17 ; ii. 12. 424 a 18 ; Ibn Rushd : T. al-Nafs ed. Ahwāni, pp. 62. 17 : 65, 15, Hyd. p. 57, 62.

(2) Ibn Sīna defines ظن , assumption, as preponderant belief, with the admission that the contrary may be the case : cf. Shīfā, Fol. 192 a 3 : والظن هوالاعتقاد والميل اليه مع تجوز الطرف الثانی

(3) Cf. Arist. De An. iii. 3. 427 a 21.
Ibn Sīna defines رأی, opinion, as firm belief ; Shīfā, Fol. 192 a 3. فالرای هوالاعتقاد المجزوم به -

(4) Cf. Arist. De An. iii. 3. 427 b 6 ; 428 a 25 ; Ibn Rushd : T. al-Nafs, ed. Ahwāni, p. 59, Hyd, p. 53 ; Pers. MS. Fol. 49 a 11 :
پس یادکرد مردمانی را وهم را قوتی پنداشتند از رای و حس محمود مرکب، وگفت نه چنانست از انکه اگر مرکب بودی از حس ورای محمود با یستی که حس ورای محمود کارکردندی در یک چیز درسفیدو سیاه و مانه چنین همی بینم ...

(5) In the second figure of syllogism the two premises must be different in quale (i. e. one must be affirmative and the other negative), and the major premiss must be universal. Its conclusive classes are four—the fourth class consists of a negative particular minor and an affirmative universal major, and gives, like the third class, a negative particular conclusion, as : some C (men) are not B (fair) ; and every A (European) is B ; therefore some C is not A ; or some imaginations cannot be verified ; all opinions can be verified ; therefor some imaginations are not opinion.

(6) Cf Arist. De An. iii. 3. 427 b 17; Ibn Rushd, T. al-Nafs Ahwāni, 60 Hyd. 55.

(7) Cf. Arist. De An. ii. 5. 417 b 20—24.

(8) Cf. Arist. De An. iii. 3. 428 a 6, Ibn Rushd: T. al. al-Nafs. Ahwāni, 59. 10, Hyd. 54. 5.

(9) Cf. Ibn Sina: Shifā, fol. 160 a12: افعال النفس ثلاثة : افعال تشترک فيهاالحيوان والنبات كالتغذية والتربية والتوليد، وافعال تشترک فيها الحيوانات جلها ولاحظ فيها النبات مثل الاحساس والتخيل والحركة الارادية

(10) Cf. Arist. iii. 3. 428 a 11; Ibn Rushd, T. al-Nafs, p. 60, Hyd. p. 54.

(11) Cf. Tadbir, ed. Asin Palacios, P. 72 : واماالتى توجد عن العقل الفاعل فكلها صادقة بالذات لابالعرض ، وكذلك ما يوجد عن الفكر الصادق ، وهذه الصور ليست صور الاجسام بعينها فتكون خاصة ولا هى ايضا مجردة عن الهيولى فتكون معقولات عامة، وليس توجد لها النسبة الخاصة ولاتوجد لها حالات المعقولات العامة ، بل توجد بين الصور الخاصة والمعقولات

(12) Cf. Arist. De Memoria et Remi, I. 449 b 31 ; 450 a 10 sq. The treatise *De Memoria* appears as the second book of the *De Sensu et Sensato* in the Arabic Compendium of Ibn Rushd as well, in the Arabic original and in all the MSS. of its Hebrew translation which have been examined ; cf. Averroes Cordubensis Compendia Librorum Aristotelis qui Parva Naturalia Vocuntur edd. Shields-Blumberg (The Medieval Academy of America, Cambridge MSS., 1949), p. 47.

(13) Cf. Ibn Rushd : T. al-Nafs, Ahwani, p. 64. 13, Hyd., p. 59.

(14) Cf. Arist. De Somniis, 2. 459 b 8-9 ; 460b 1 ; Ibn Rushd : T. Nafs, 63.

(15) Cf. Arist. De Memoria, 1. 450 b 18; De Somniis, 3. 461b1.

(16) Cf. Arist. De Somniis, 2.458 b 26-29 : 3. 460 b 29-30, Al-Fārābi and Ibn Sina use الممرورون , the bilious, and المحرورون, the fever-patients, instead of المرسمين , the hallucinators or designers ; see Al-Madīnat al-Fāḍila, ed. Dieterici, p. 53 ; Shīfa Fol. 180 a 19 : والصورة اذاكانت فى الحس المشترك كانت محسوسة بالحقيقة فيها حتى اذا انطبع فيها صورة كاذبة فى الوجود احسته كما يعرض للمحرورين .

(17) Ibn Bāj. refers to the case of " hallucination ". Cf. Ibn Sina, Fol. 183 b . فان شغلت المتخيلة من الجهتين جميعا ضعف فعلها ، وان زال عنها الشغل من الجهتين كلتيهما كما يكون فى حال النوم ، او من جهة واحدة كما يكون عندالامراض ...... وكما عندالخوف ... وقوع امور جسدانية ... فتلوح الصورالتى فى المصورة فى الحاس المشترك ، فترى كانها موجودة خارجا

(18) Cf. Arist. De Somniis, 3. 462 a 10-14 ; Ibn Sina, Shifa, fol. I83b: ولهذا مايرى الانسان المجنون والخايف والضعيف والنايم اشباحا قايمة كما تراها فى حال السلامة بالحقيقة ويسمع اصواتا كذلك .

(19) Cf. Arist. De Somniis, 2.460b 5-25.

(20) Cf. Arist. De Somniis, 2.459a 25-27.

(21) Cf. Zeller: Plato (trans. Alleyne and Goodwin), p. 239; Republic x. 596A/Ritter, ii. 306; 303A3.

(22) Cf. Arist. De Somniis, 2.459b I-5 (qualitative change)

(23) Ibid. 3.46Ib I6-24 (The residuary movements are like these).

(24) Cf. Arist. De An. iii. 4.430a 7.

(25) Cf. Arist. De Memoria, I.450a 11-I4.

(26) Cf. Arist. De Memoria, I.45Ia8.

(27) Cf. Arist. De Somniis, 3.462a I3-I4.

(28) Cf. Arist. De Somniis et Vigilia, 3.456 b I0-I6; 457a9. See Note I7.

(29) Cf. Arist. De An. iii. 4.429 a 3I-b4; De Somniis, 2.459 b I0-22; Ibn Rushd: T. al-Nafs, Ahwani, p. 154. I7-22.

(30) Cf. Arist. De An. iii. 10. 433 a 20

(31) Cf. Arist. De An. iii .429a5; Ibn Sina, Shifā, Fol. 191 a 25:
وللحيوانات الاخرى وخصوصا للطير صناعات ايضا فانها تصنع بيوتا وساكن لاسيما النحل لكن ذلک ليس ممايصدر عن استنباط و قياس بل عن الهام وتسخير ولذلک ليس مما يختلف ويتنوع واكثرها لصلاح انواعها وللضرورية النوعية وليست للضرورة الشخصية .
also Fol. I9Ib5 : وربما وقع هذا العارض فى الجبلة ومن الالهام الالهى كحب كل حيوان ولده من غير اعتقاد البتة بل على نوع تخيل بعض الانسان لشى نافع او لذيذ ونفرته عنه ......
Ibn Rushd: T. al-Nafs, Ahwani, p. 71.

(32) Cf. Arist. Phys. viii. 256 a 20.

(33) Cf. Ibn Rushd: T. al-Nafs, Ahwani, p. 74. He uses قريب and بعيد instead of اول and ثانى .

(34) 'To perceive a particular' means 'to perceive a form in its matter' see Ibn Rushd: T. al-Nafs, p. 67, Hyd. p. 62.

(35) Cf. Text, Fol. 154 A, Damascus, p. 97

(36) Cf. Arist. De An. iii. 7.431a 14-19.

(37) To perceive a universal means to perceive a common form as separated from matter, and sense-perception and

imagination perceive only those forms that are in matter; see Ibn Rushd T. al-Nafs, p. 67, Hyd. p. 63.

(38) Cf. Arist. De An. iii. 6.430b 5; Ibn Sīna, Fol. 183a (Shifa):
وان الحس المشترك يودى الى القوة المصورة على سبيل استخزان ما يودى اليها الحواس فتخنزنه وقد تخزن القوة المصورة ايضا اشياء ليست من الماخوذات عن الحس ، فان القوة المفكرة قد تتصرف ... بالتركيب والتحكيل .
Ibn Rushd: T. al-Nafs, p. 68.3, Hyd. p. 63.7.

(39) Cf. Arist. De Somniis, 2.459 a 23 sq.

(40) Cf. Arist. De An. iii 8.432 a 3-10.

(41) Cf. Arist. Met. Z. vii. 1035 b 29.

(42) Cf. Arist. Met. A. i. 991 b 3.

——:o:——

CHAPTER XI

DISCOURSE ON THE REASONING FACULTY

The faculty of reason is neither always actual, since knowledge is not recollection — and our knowledge is not perfect — nor always potential, because man acquires knowledge by perception or by learning. It is, therefore, sometimes potential sometimes actual.

It is through this faculty that a man understands a man, and achieves or imparts knowledge. This faculty has, therefore, an organ through which man expresses himself and composes different meanings in the form of a definite speech.

The meanings indicated by words are either universals or particulars — the particulars are apprehended by the faculty of imagination, and the universals are common to all arts and sciences. These universals are intelligible meanings and are either eternal or transitory.

(1) Cf. Ibn Rushd : T. al-Nafs, Ahwāni, p. 81.18.

(2) Ibid. p. 66.16.

(3) Ibid. p. 80-2.

(4) Whereas ' no one can learn ... in the absence of sense', *see* Arist. De An iii 8.432a6.

(5) Cf. Ibn Rushd: T. al-Nāfs, Ahwāni p. 79.9.

(6) Cf. Ibn Bāj. fol. 135a : القوةالمتخيلة الموجودة فى الانسان بالفعل هى القوةالتى يجدها الانسان فى نفسه يرسم فيها رسوم المحسوسات ويتصور بها ويحضر للانسان فيها رسوم من المحسوسات متخيلة بعد غيبتها عن الحواس فيرى الانسان فيها صفة زيد و عمر و: وصفة داره و ذاته وغير ذلك من المحسوسات المشار اليها -

(7) This verse belongs to a قصيده (ode) by Abū Qays Ibn al-Ṣalt and has been quoted by al-Sibawayh in his *Kitāb* (ed. Hartwig Derenbourg, Paris, I. p. 322), Ibn Manẓūr in his *Lisān* (under حرف القاف , p. 231 al-Baghdādī in his *Khizāna*, vol. ii. p. 45, iii. p. 144.

(8) Cf. Ibn Rushd : T. al-Nafs, Ahwāni, p. 66 : انها انما تتعطل, افعالها فى الصبا لانها مغمورة بالرطوبة —

Ibn Bāj., al-Ittiṣāl (published by Ahwāni along with Talkhīs K. al-Nafs l' Ibn Rushd, p. 107) : و هى موجودة فى الطفل وغيرتها الرطوبة او تحدث باخرة

(9) Cf. Ibn Bāj. Fol. 199a 10 : والقول التام اجناسه عند كثير من القدماء خمسة : جازم وتضرع ، وطلبة و نداء ، لانه قد يمكن ان يوجد بطريق اخر فيكون اكثر ، والتمنى وما يجرى مجراه جار مجرى الجازم لانه لم يتغير فيه الجازم بل يقر على حاله زيادة

(10) Cf. Ibn Bāj. Fol. 135a : وكذلك وجود القوة الناطقة يجدهاالانسان فى نفسه ويعلمها علما يقينا لا يشك فيه شيئى من التثبت و ذلك انا نجد انفسنا ما يتميز به ويفصل عن ساير الحيوان المتغذى الحساس ، فانالانسان يجد فى نفسه معلومات يحتوى على ميز الجميل و القبيح و النافع و الضار . . . و يميزها و يجد فى نفسه ' امو رايرى صدقها لا يشك فيه اسورا على ما هى ظن ، واموراهى كذب لا يجوز فى الوجود كل هذه المعلومات يجدها الانسان فى نفسه وهذه المعانى المعلومة فى النفس يسمى نطقا ، و ما يوجد فى الانسان يسمى ناطقا

(11) Cf. Ibn Rushd : T. al-Nafs, Ahwāni, p. 67. 10, Hyd. p. 62.13.

(12) Ibid. 68. I, Hyd. 63.15.

(13) Ibid. p. 80.19, Hyd. 77.6.

——:o:——

BIBLIOGRAPHY

Abū Rida Muḥammad 'Abd al-Hādi : Rasā'il al-Kindi.

Ahlwardt, W. : Verzeichniss Der Arabischen Handschriften Der Koniglichen Bibliothek Zu Berlin, vierter Band VII und VIII Buch, Berlin, 1892.

Al-Ahwāni, Aḥmad Fu'ād : Talkhīṣ Kitab al-Nafs li Abi 'l-Walīd Ibn Rushd, K. al-Nafs al-Mansūb li' Isḥāq Risālat al-'Ittiṣāl li 'Ibn Bājja, Egypt, 1950.

Al-Andalus, Granad—Madrid : See Asin Palacios.

'Ali al-Thānawi : Kashshāf 'Iṣṭilāḥāt al-Funūn, ed. Sprenger.

Aristotle : The works of Aristotle translated into English, ed. W. D. Ross.

The Calcutta MS. entitled "Risālat li 'l-Arisṭāṭālīs fi al-Nafs".

The Bodl. MS. Ousl. 92, "Risāla dar Nafs mansūbba Arisṭāṭālīs".

Asin Palacios, M. : Tratado de Avempace Sobre la union del intelecto con el hombre, Al Andalus, vol. 7. 1942, 1-47.

La "Carta de Adios" de Avempace, Al Andalus, vol. 8, 1943, 1-87.

Kitāb al-Nabāt, Al Andalus, vol. 5, 1940, 266-78. Tadbīr al-Mutawaḥḥid li 'Ibn Bājjah.

Kitāb al-Ḥadā'iq li Ibn al-Sid, Al Andalus, vol. 5, 1940, 63-98.

Badawi, 'Abdur-Raḥmān : Arisṭū 'Indal-'Arab.

Bergsträsser : Galeni in Hippocratis De Septimanis.

Bouyges, M. : See Ibn Rus͟hd and al-Fārābi.

Brockelmann, C. : Geschichte der Arabischen Literatur, in two volumes, Supplementband in three volumes.

Dieterici, F. : Al-Fārābi's philosophische Abhandlungen, Leiden, 1890.

Dunlop, D. M. : Ibn Bājjah's Tadbiru'l-Mutawaḥḥid (Rule of the Solitary). JRAS, 1945, 61-81.

The *Encyclopaedia of Islam*, ed. Houtsma, Arnold, Basset and Hartmann Leyden, 1913, four volumes, and Suppl.

Faḍl al-Raḥmān : Avicenna's Psychology, a D. Phil. thesis in the Bodleian Library.

Al-Fārābi, Abu Naṣr Muḥammad Ibn Tark͟hān : Fuṣūl al-Madani, the Bodl. MS. Hunt. 307.
Fuṣuṣ al Ḥikam, ed. Dieterici.
Iḥṣā'ul-'Ulūm, Madrid, 1932.
Masā'il Mutafarriqa, Hyderabad.
Al-Madīnat al-Faḍilat, ed. Dieterici.
Al-Siyāsāt al-Madaniyah, Hyderabad.

Flugel, G. : See Ibn al-Nadīm.

Galen : See Bergsträsser and Kraus-Walzer.

Gauthier, L. : Roman philosphique d 'Ibn Ṭufayl, text et traduction, Beyrouth, 1936.

Goichon, A. M. : Lexique de la langue philosophique d 'Ibn Sina, Paris, 1938.
Vocabulaires compares d'Aristote et d 'Ibn Sina, Supplement au Lexique de la langue philosophique.

Ibn Bājjah : The Bodleian MS. Pocock 206 entitled "Majmū'at min Kalām Ibn Bājjah"; see Asin Palacios.

Ibn Khaldūn : Tārīkh, vol. I, Bulāq.

Ibn Khallikān : Wafayāt al-'A'yān.

Ibn al-Nadīm : Kitāb al-Fihrist, ed. Flugel, Leipzig, 1871.

Ibn al-Qifṭī : Tārikh al-Hukamā', ed. J. Lippert, Leipzig, 1903.

Ibn Rushd : Talkhīṣ K. al-Nafs, ed. al-Ahwāni.
Rasā'il Ibn Rushd, Ḥyderabad, 1946.
Tafsīr Mā Ba'd al-Ṭabī 'ah, ed. Bouyges, 3 vols.
Kitāb al-Kulliyāt, Artes Graficas, Bosca, Larache, Marruecos, 1939.

Ibn al-Sīd al-Baṭalyawsi : Kitāb al-Ḥadā'iq, see Asin Palacios.

Ibn Sina : Kitāb al-Shifā', The Bodl. MS. Poc. 125.
Ta'līqāt K. al-Nafs, ed. 'Abd al-Rahmān Badawi, 'Arisuṭū 'ind al-'Arab.

Ibn Ṭufayl : Ḥayy Ibn Yaqẓān, ed. Gauthier.
English translation by Simon Ockley, reprinted by Edward A. Van Dyck, Cairo, 1905.

Jowett, A. Dialogues of Plato translated into English, 5 vols.

JRAS : Journal of the Royal Asiatic Society, London.

Al-Kindi : See Abu Rida.

Kraus-Walzer : Galenic Compendium Timaei Platonis, London, 1951.

Lane, E. : Arabic-English Lexicon.

Makkenna : Plotinus, Enneads, translated into English, 4 vols.

Al-Maqqari, Aḥmad : Nafḥ al-Ṭīb, 4 vols.

Müller, A. : ed. Ibn 'Abī 'Uṣaibi' ah's 'Uyūn al-'Anbā' fi Ṭabaqāt al-Aṭibbā', Konigsburg & Cairo, 1882-4.

Ockley, S. : Philosophus Autodidactus or Hayy Ibn Yaqzan. See Ibn Tufayl.

Pocock, E. : Philosophus Autodidactus, Elenchos Scriptorum.

Ross, W. D. : see Aristotle.

Sarton, G. Introduction to the History of Science, 2 vols. in 3 parts, Baltimor, 1927-31.

Sprenger : See Ali al-Thanawi.

Walzer, R. : See Kraus.

Wright : Arabic Grammar (Engl.), 2 vols.

Zeller, E. : Aristotle and Earlier Peripatetics, translated into Eng. by Contelloc and Muirhead, 2 vols.

———:o:———

APPENDIX
AN ABSTRACT
OF
IBN BĀJJAH'S PARAPHRASE OF ARISTOTLE'S *DE ANIMA*

The Kitāb al-Nafs of Abū Bakr Muḥammad Ibn Yaḥyā al-Ṣā'igh known as Ibn Bājjah (d. 533/1138) is the earliest Arabic text so far known that gives us an elaborate paraphrase of the *De Anima* of Aristotle. This book which was never edited before has survived through Abu 'l-Ḥasan Ibn al-Imām, a close friend and favourite student of Ibn Bājjah, who collected all the writings of his master in a single volume. There are two MSS. of this volume known preserved in the libraries of Oxford and Berlin. But the Berlin MS. which was shifted to the Eastern part of Germany during the last Great War is lost, as I learned from the Berlin Librarian. I have, therefore, based my edition of this book on the Oxford manuscript alone.

Besides editing the text, I have prepared an English translation and have added explanatory notes, where necessary. In the translation an attempt has been made to be literal and to keep close to the text. For convenience of the readers the text has been divided into separate paragraphs.

Since the MS. is seven centuries old, partly slightly damaged, and very often without diacritical points, and full of errors, the editor has had to decipher carefully the whole MS. which contains 222 folios—and that in order to establish the text, and restore the damaged portions and lacunas.

In the commentary, besides quoting parallel passages from Ibn Bājjah's other works, I have traced the origin of his psychological views in the *De Anima*, and other Aristotelian and Greek works as well. I have also compared this work with the works of Ibn Bājjah's Muslim predecessors, particularly with those of also Al-Fārābī (d. 339/950), and Ibn Sīna (d. 428/1037), and with the writings of Ibn Rus͟hd (d. 595/1198), his pupil.

Ibn Bājjah exerted a great influence on his contemporary thinkers, Ibn Ṭufayl (d. 581/1185) and Ibn Rus͟hd in particular, and on the Latin scholars of the Middle Ages in general. His Latinized name, *Avempace*, seems to have been very popular among the Hebrew and Latin scholars in those days. His treatises, the *Tadbīr al-Mutawaḥḥid*, the *Risālat al-Ittiṣāl*, and the *Risālat al-Wadā'*, were widely read in the then Europe, and exist in Hebrew translations. The Arabic text of these treatises was, for the first time, edited by late Professor Asin Palacios of Spain. A few pages of the *K. Tadbīr al-Mutawaḥḥid* with English translation were published by Mr. D. M. Dunlop of Cambridge in the *Journal of the Royal Asiatic Society*, 1945. But the *Kitāb al-Nafs* seems to have never been translated into Latin or Hebrew.

In the introduction, I have thrown light on the importance of this book, and on the style of Ibn Bājjah's exposition of philosophical problems as well. I have also described the manuscript. Besides, I have tried to give a brief survey of the psychological views of Ibn Bājjah.

Since a few pages from the end of the text were lost in the very days of Ibn al-Imām, it is difficult to make sure which conclusion Ibn Bājjah has reached in this book. The text in hand, however, clearly agrees with the main arguments discussed in the second and third books of Aristotle's *De Anima*. The same definition of Soul as advanced by Aristotle in his *De Anima*—the first entelechy of an organized body—has been accepted and the same difficulty in explaining the connection of the "intellect" and the animate body that arises in the *De Anima* has been evidently realized in this book as well. But Ibn Bājjah, like Al-Fārābī and Ibn Sīna, who have always been trying to explain the close affinity between reason and revelation on a rational basis, strives rather in his own Islāmic way to solve this difficulty through introducing the theory of revelation which he propounds in the *Risālat al-'Ittiṣāl* and a few other small treatises on Appetition and Active Intellect which have not yet been published, and which can together easily form a second part of this book.

In the end, I must confess that there are a number of obscure passages in the text which in spite of my best efforts I have not quite understood. There might be some lacunas somewhere in these passages which the editor has failed to guess, and which might probably be supplied by the other manuscript, if it ever turns up again, and thus render them easy to understanding.

But for the importance of the work in the history of the science of Soul in the Muslim World, and in the world at large, this work would have been left undone. Nevertheless, it is expected that this first edition of Ibn Bājjah's *Kitāb al-Nafs* will to an extent facilitate the task of its second edition in future.

As I am not well up in Greek I have relied on the Oxford translation of the works of Aristotle and on the English translation of other Greek works.

INDEX

A

Abū Naṣr : 51, 54; also see Farabi.
Accidental : 14, 16.
Acquired Intellect : 33, 53, 143, 147.
Active Mind : 7.
—— faculty : 8.
Actual : 49.
Actual intellect : 55, 144.
Aggregate : 49, 69.
Ahlwardt : 10, 11.
al-Ahwāni, Ahmad Fu'ād : 5.
Alexander of Aphrodisias : 4, 5, 10, 25, 92, 178, 181.
'Āli ibn al-Imām : 2, 4, 5, 10, 11, 12, 177.
Alteration : 128, 146, 147.
Anaxagoras : 141.
Ants : 111.
Appetition : 7.
Appetitive Soul . 9.
Apprehensions : 158.
Aqmeous : 119.
Ariston : 5.
Aristotle : 2, 4, 5, 6, 7, 8, 13, 17, 21, 24, 26, 27, 51, 52, 62, 82, 100, 114, 115, 125, 126, 127, 128, 129, 130, 131, 132, 133, 136, 137, 138, 142, 145, 146, 149, 150, 154, 156, 163, 173, 176, 177, 179, 181, 182, 183.
Aromatic : 95.
Arrangement : 41.
Arsenic : 95.
Art : 15, 16, 36, 40.
Artisan : 47.
Artificial bodies : 13, 14, 16, 130.
Asin Palacios, Prof. : 11, 127, 148.
Assumption : 106.
Automatic : 15, 132.
Averrocs : 1. See also Ibn Rushd.
Axiomatic : 20.

B

Bājjah, Ibn : 1, 2, 3, 4, 5, 6, 7, 8, 9, 10, 12, 125, 126, 127, 128, 129, 130, 131, 132, 133, 134, 135, 138, 141, 142, 145, 146, 147, 148, 150, 151, 153, 154, 156, 163, 164, 167, 171, 181, 182.
Bamm : 88.
Becoming : 61, 83.
Bee : 69, 111.
Being : 143, 146.
Best being : 52.
Bitter : 96.
Boat : 105.
Body : 17, 43, 50, 51.
Book of Animals : 35, 38, 40 41, 50, 62, 67, 77, 82, 102, 105.

Book of Plants : 35.
Broiling : 94, 95, 178.

C

Captain : 105, 186.
Categories : 31, 146.
Causes : 86.
Change : 30, 43, 49, 54, 55,
—— in being : 55, 61, 76, 83, 128, 131, 146, 169, 174.
Coldness, psychical : 100.
Colour : 80, 81, 86, 92, 172.
Common Sense : 103, 104, 108, 185.
Composition, method of : 23, 62.
Concoction : 64.
Condensation : 64, 69.
Connection : 49, 50, 54, 55, 61.
Continuation : 41.
Continuous : 46, 48.
Contraries : 46, 83.
Contrariety : 46.
Contrivance : 56.
Corruption : 44, 130.
Cricket : 90.
Curtain : 93, 179.

D

De Anima : 2, 4, 5, 26.
Definition : 19, 20, 21, 22, 25.
De Generatione et Corruptione: 38, 39, 63, 98.
Democritus : 21, 86, 126, 127.
De Sensu et Sensatu : 81, 85, 94, 95, 107, 108, 109, 110.
Desire, natural : 9
Dieterici : 127.
Differentia : 22.
Dimensions : 59.
Divine Gift : 8.
Division, method of : 23, 25.
Dry : 96.
Duntop, D. M. : 1, 11.

E

Element : 13, 14, 19, 57.
Empedocles : 141.
Entelechy, definition : 15, 17, 25, 31, 79, 125, 131, 134, 135.
Essential : 14.
Existence : 52, 56.
Extension : 59, 82.
Eye : 80.

F

Faculty of Generation : 27.
—— of moving : 33.
—— of imagination : 114.
—— of nutrition : 33.
—— of growth : 42.
—— of reason : 56.
False : 107.
al-Farabi : 3, 4, 5, 6, 7, 9, 92, 126, 127, 138, 140, 141, 164, 165, 189.
Fever : 96.
Fire : 82.
First : 79, 81.
First entelechy : 17.
—— mover : 14, 15, 163.
—— principle : 19.
Flavour : 96.
Flesh : 98, 101.
Flux : 100.

Food : 33, 34, 35, 36, 39, 56, 148, 150.
Form : 7, 13, 15, 16, 17, 19, 43, 44, 48, 49, 51, 53, 54, 56, 57, 60, 61, 66, 69, 70, 71, 72, 74, 77, 103, 105, 125, 127, 138, 147, 159, 162, 163.
Fragrance : 95.
Fuṣūl al-Madani : 126.
Fuṣūṣ : 7.

G

Galen : 5, 21, 62, 99, 100, 126, 127.
Generation : 14, 27, 43, 92, 131, 149, 168.
Generative faculty : 37, 40, 154.
Generator : 36.
Genesis : 128.
Genus : 21, 22, 23, 24, 35, 36, 52, 54, 138.
al-Ghazzāli : 6, 19.
Gift, Divine : 8.
Growth : 143.

H

Hallucination : 189.
al-Hasan : see Ibn al-Naḍar.
Hearing : 88, 176.
Heat : 38, 63, 68, 95, 152.
Heaven and Earth : 51.
Homogeneous : 45, 55, 60.
not homogeneous : 45.
Ḥunayn : 5, 127, 173.

I

Ibn Bājjah : see Bājjah.
Ibn al-Biṭrīq : 5.
—— al-Imām : see 'Ali.
—— al-Nadīm : 5.
—— al-Naḍar : 10.
—— Rus͟hd : 4, 5, 126, 127, 136, 138, 142, 144, 147, 148, 150, 156, 159, 171, 173, 181.
Ibn Sina : 1, 4, 5, 6, 7, 9, 127, 136, 139, 140, 152, 153, 154, 170, 183, 186, 188, 189.
—— Isḥāq : 127.
—— Ibn Ṭufayl : 2, 3, 4, 12.
Iḥṣā' al-'Ulūm : 126.
Illuminant : 81, 83, 84, 86.
Illumination : 84, 86.
Imagination : 8, 27, 76, 106, 109, 110, 187.
Imaginative : 17.
—— Faculty : 8, 110, 111, 113.
Impinging : 88.
—— appetition : 7.
Inclination : 48.
Inhale : 93.
Innate heat : 100, 104, 105, 38.
Intelligence : 51.
Intellectual Faculty : 153.
Instrument : 14, 17.
Intention : 37, 38, 57, 95.
Intermediate appetition : 7.
Isḥāq : 5, 150, 156.

J

Juggler : 90.
Juniper : 95.

K

Kahle, P. E. : 1.

Knowledge : 17, 18, 19, 20, 21, 24.

L

Last : 79.
—— entelechy : 17.
Learning : 117.
Light : 81, 85, 86.
Lip, broad : 102.
Logos : 118.
Lute : 89.

M

Mathematical Sights and Shades : 82.
Mathlath : 88.
Mathna . 88.
Matter : 8, 13, 19, 43, 44, 46, 47, 48, 49, 51, 55, 56, 58, 59, 60, 66, 70, 71, 74, 103, 108, 110, 112, 138, 159, 162.
Meaning : 72, 75.
Medium : 99, 100.
Metaphysics : 18, 22, 33, 48, 115.
Meteorology : 63, 65, 67.
Mind : 9, 153.
Mineral bodies : 64, 65.
Mirror : 87.
Mixing : 63, 64, 69, 92, 168, 178.
Mixture : 62, 63, 95.
Moist : 88, 96.
Moisture : 95, 96.
Motion: 15, 44, 130, 147.
Moved : 16, 47, 62, 161.
Movent : 102.
Moving faculty : 34, 37.
Movement : 39, 55, 66, 87, 88, 133.
Mover : 14, 15, 16, 32, 35, 36, 45, 47, 54, 55, 56, 60, 62, 63, 65, 75, 100, 127, 128, 133, 160, 161.
Musk : 95.
Muṭlaq : 88.

N

Nature : 16, 17, 34, 51.
Natural bodies : 13, 14, 16, 17, 127.
—— body : 39, 132.
—— things : 126.
—— desire : 9.
Nutritive faculty, definition : 6, 29, 35, 39, 40.
—— soul : 17, 35, 38, 42, 133, 148, 149.
Necessary, definition : 29.
Nerve : 100.
Nourishment : 56.
Nutrient : 35.

O

Ockley : 12.
Odorous : 95.
Odour : 92, 93, 94, 95.
Oesophagus : 90.
Opinion : 106.
Organ : 98, 99, 100.

P

Particular : 77, 120, 192.
Passive faculty : 8, 143.
Passivity : 31.
Paul Karaus : 127.

Perception, definition : 7, 8. 57, 101, 187.
Perfection : 15, 17, 56.
Peri Hermenias : 119.
Peripatetics : 52.
Per prius et posterims : 19.
Phaedo : 115.
Phantom : 108.
Philosophische Abhandlungden : 127.
Physics : 26, 29, 30, 38, 43, 49, 50, 58, 67, 69, 70, 76, 83, 111, 127.
Plato : 5, 21, 26, 48, 52, 109, 115, 126, 137, 161.
Pleuritics : 107.
Plotinus : 160
Plutarch : 5.
Pneuma, innate : 100.
Pocock, E : 10, 12.
Politics, the Science of : 15, 132.
Political Science : 18.
Possible : 143, 144.
Posterior Analytics : 20, 21, 22.
Position : 31, 83.
Possession : 31.
Potentiality : 33, 44, 46, 48, 58, 62, 73, 110.
Principle, First : 19.
Prime mover : 47.
Privation : 144.
Prophecy : 9.
Psychical coldness : 100.
——— perception : 158.
Psychology : 18, 125.
Putridity : 41.

Q

Quantity : 31, 34.
Quality : 31.

R

Rarefaction : 64.
Rational Appetition : 7.
——— faculty : 8.
Reasoning faculty : 8, 117, 118, 192.
——— Soul : 17.
Recollection : 117.
Representation : 108, 109, 112, 114.
Reproduction : 7, 41, 143, 144.
Relation, category of : 31, 83, 84.
Reproductive faculty : 39, 40, 42, 57.
Respiration : 93.
Revelation : 9.

S

al-Sā'igh, Ibn : 1.
Sabbāba : 88.
Sensation : 8, 56, 62, 106, 110, 158.
Sensible : 107.
—— Book on : 114.
Sense : 102, 103.
Sensitive : 17.
Sense perception : 43, 57, 58, 66, 76, 77, 87, 91, 98, 103, 107, 108, 157.
Sentient : 62.
Separation : 112.

Shadow : 87.
Shell : 97.
Shiga : 127.
Sight : 79, 101, 172.
Signs : 20.
Simplicius : 5.
Simple being : 13.
Skin : 98, 99.
Sleep : 105, 110.
Smell : 92, 95, 178.
Smoke : 82, 96.
Sound : 89, 176.
Soul, definition : 6, 7, 8, 16, 17, 18, 20, 21, 22, 23, 24, 25, 26, 32, 38, 42, 54, 56, 61, 79, 104, 125, 133, 156.
Space : 31.
Sperm : 41, 42.
Spherical body : 51, 55, 147.
Sponge : 97, 148.
Spontaneous growth : 155.
Stick : 101.
Storax : 95.
Substance : 31, 140.
Substratum : 30, 31, 51, 57, 83, 160.
Succession : 41.
Successive : 156.
Syllogism : 23.

T

Tadbīr al-Mutawaḥḥid : 1, 2, 11, 12, 127, 132. 134.
Tangible : 62, 98, 101, 182.
Taste : 93, 96, 181
Terrestrial : 81.
Themislius : 5, 101, 181, 184.
Theophrastus : 5.
Thunder : 90.
Throat : 96.
Timaeus : 21, 127.
Time : 31.
Touch : 98, 99, 101, 182.
Transformation : 14, 110.
Transitory : 73.
Translucence : 86.
Translucent : 86.
Transitory movement : 32.
True : 107.
Trunk : 102.

U

Universal : 120, 190, 192.
Urula : 96.

V

Viscous : 96.
Vision : 79, 86, 173.
Vitreous humour : 173.

W

Walzer, R. : 127.
Wood : 44, 45, 46, 47.

Z

Zīr : 88, 89.

CORRIGENDA

P .5 :	*Read* (at the end) : يقين يمتاز به اقاويلهم	instead of	. . . يمتاز بدٌ اقاويلم
P. 38. 2 :	,, "being"	instead of	being.
P. 50.23 :	,, Now	,,	New
P. 57.23 :	,, later on	,,	latter on
,, 30 :	,, by what	,,	by when
P. 58.6 :	,, of smell	,,	of small
,, 11 :	,, mouth	,,	month
P. 63 28 :	,, inefficient	,,	in efficient
P. 8[illegible].21 :	,, As though	,,	As through
P. 127.1 & 4	,, العاسية	,,	العاسيتة
P. 128.25 :	,, accidentally	,,	accidentlly
P. 129.2 :	,, بالا بعد فالا بعد		بالا بعد فابعد

,, . 13-14 : Read : (من المتوسطات من المحرک , a. MS ; منها . . .
Fol. 48 a : وان المحرک والمتحرک ... بطريق العرض ... المحركة بذاتها
Fol. 50 a. : و المحرک ينفصل بتقابل يخصه و هو ان يحرک بنفسه . . .
و قد يحرک بغيره

P. 129.26 : *Read* : زيد هنا ان المحرک القريب عندما يبتدئ بالحركة يلي المتحرک

al-Kawn, Fol. 81 b : فالمحرک اذا حرک المحرک فقد ماس هذا المحرک بطبيعة ذلک المتحرک و المتحرک ممسوس .

Fol. 82 b : ان كل متحرک فهو يتلوا محركه الا قرب ضرورة . . . فالمتحرک والمحرک يتماسان

P. 131.15-16 : *Read* : و اما الذي يبقى فيه المتغير ؛ Fol. 16 a , متى لم يوجو لم يكن ذالک الوجود واحدا بعينه فظاهر . . . من الجهل الى العلم سمى استكمالا

Fol. 16 b. فالكون و الفساد ليسا بحركتين . . . اذاهى لموجود بالكمال ومن وجود بالكمال و الى موجود بالكمال .

P. 131.35 : *Read* : ولا يبارحه حتى instead of ولا يبارح حد حق

P.132 (second line from bottom) : *Read* :

Fol. 182 a : و ان يكون الذي يتخيل الوانا ما مشمول العين

Fol. 183 b 22 . . . سببها اتصالات مالا يشعر بها

P. 134-12 : ن تلقايه و اذا ذهب هذا الروح عند موت الحيوان بقيت تلک (المتوسطات) غير متحركة ولا محركة

Al-Ḥayawān, Fol. 96 a : فهناک النفس والآلة الاولى على ما تلخص في الرابعة الخ

P. 135.24 & 25 : *Read* : "See the Ar. Text Fol. 155 A, Damascus, p. 101 : ان النفس هى الاستكمال الاول

P. 137.4 : Al-'Āthār al-'Ulwiyah Fol. 71 b فان الحدود كما قيل فى انالوطيقى تولف . . . الخ

P. 138.6-7: *Read* : " . . . هذا العلم مزمعان . . . " ; " ان كان مزمعا ان يجرى "

P. 175. No: 26 : *Read* : "المرآة" instead of 'المرءة"